THE OEDIPUS PLAYS

Sophocles

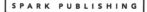

SPARK PUBLISHING

SPARKNOTES is a registered trademark of SparkNotes LLC

Spark Publishing
A Division of Barnes & Noble
120 Fifth Avenue
New York, NY 10011
www.sparknotes.com

ISBN-13: 978-1-4114-0360-4
ISBN-10: 1-4114-0360-6

Please submit changes or report errors to www.sparknotes.com/errors.

Printed in the United States.

10 9 8 7 6

Contents

Context

Greek Theater

GREEK THEATER WAS VERY DIFFERENT from what we call theater today. It was, first of all, part of a religious festival. To attend a performance of one of these plays was an act of worship, not entertainment or intellectual pastime. But it is difficult for us to even begin to understand this aspect of the Greek theater, because the religion in question was very different from modern religions. The god celebrated by the performances of these plays was Dionysus, a deity who lived in the wild and was known for his subversive revelry. The worship of Dionysus was associated with an ecstasy that bordered on madness. Dionysus, whose cult was that of drunkenness and sexuality, little resembles modern images of God.

A second way in which Greek theater was different from modern theater is in its cultural centrality: every citizen attended these plays. Greek plays were put on at annual festivals (at the beginning of spring, the season of Dionysus), often for as many as 15,000 spectators at once. They dazzled viewers with their special effects, singing, and dancing, as well as with their beautiful language. At the end of each year's festivals, judges would vote to decide which playwright's play was the best.

In these competitions, Sophocles was king. It is thought that he won the first prize at the Athenian festival eighteen times. Far from being a tortured artist working at the fringes of society, Sophocles was among the most popular and well-respected men of his day. Like most good Athenians, Sophocles was involved with the political and military affairs of Athenian democracy. He did stints as a city treasurer and as a naval officer, and throughout his life he was a close friend of the foremost statesman of the day, Pericles. At the same time, Sophocles wrote prolifically. He is believed to have authored 123 plays, only seven of which have survived.

Sophocles lived a long life, but not long enough to witness the downfall of his Athens. Toward the end of his life, Athens became entangled in a war with other city-states jealous of its prosperity and power, a war that would end the glorious century during which Sophocles lived. This political fall also marked an artistic fall, for the unique art of Greek theater began to fade and eventually died. Since then, we have had nothing like it. Nonetheless, we still try to read it, and we often misunderstand it by thinking of it in terms of the categories and assumptions of our own arts. Greek theater still needs to be read, but we must not forget that, because it is so alien to us, reading these plays calls not only for analysis, but also for imagination.

ANTIGONE

Antigone was probably the first of the three Theban plays that Sophocles wrote, although the events dramatized in it happen last. Antigone is one of the first heroines in literature, a woman who fights against a male power structure, exhibiting greater bravery than any of the men who scorn her. *Antigone* is not only a feminist play but a radical one as well, making rebellion against authority appear splendid and noble. If we think of *Antigone* as something merely ancient, we make the same error as the Nazi censors who allowed Jean Anouilh's adaptation of *Antigone* to be performed, mistaking one of the most powerful texts of the French Resistance for something harmlessly academic.

OEDIPUS THE KING

The story of Oedipus was well known to Sophocles' audience. Oedipus arrives at Thebes a stranger and finds the town under the curse of the Sphinx, who will not free the city unless her riddle is answered. Oedipus solves the riddle and, since the king has recently been murdered, becomes the king and marries the queen. In time, he comes to learn that he is actually a Theban, the king's son, cast out of Thebes as a baby. He has killed his father and married his mother. Horrified, he blinds himself and leaves Thebes forever.

The story was not invented by Sophocles. Quite the opposite: the play's most powerful effects often depend on the fact that the audience already knows the story. Since the first performance of *Oedipus Rex*, the story has fascinated critics just as it fascinated Sophocles. Aristotle used this play and its plot as the supreme example of tragedy. Sigmund Freud famously based his theory of the "Oedipal Complex" on this story, claiming that every boy has a latent desire to kill his father and sleep with his mother. The story of Oedipus has given birth to innumerable fascinating variations, but we should not forget that this play is one of the variations, not the original story itself.

OEDIPUS AT COLONUS

Beginning with the arrival of Oedipus in Colonus after years of wandering, *Oedipus at Colonus* ends with Antigone setting off toward her own fate in Thebes. In and of itself, *Oedipus at Colonus* is not a tragedy; it hardly even has a plot in the normal sense of the word. Thought to have been written toward the end of Sophocles' life and the conclusion of the Golden Age of Athens, *Oedipus at Colonus*, the last of the Oedipus plays, is a quiet and religious play, one that does not attempt the dramatic fireworks of the others. Written after *Antigone,* the play for which it might be seen as a kind of prequel, *Oedipus at Colonus* seems not to look forward to the suffering that envelops that play but back upon it, as though it has already been surmounted.

Plot Overview

Antigone

Antigone and ismene, the daughters of oedipus, discuss the disaster that has just befallen them. Their brothers Polynices and Eteocles have killed one another in a battle for control over Thebes. Creon now rules the city, and he has ordered that Polynices, who brought a foreign army against Thebes, not be allowed proper burial rites. Creon threatens to kill anyone who tries to bury Polynices and stations sentries over his body. Antigone, in spite of Creon's edict and without the help of her sister Ismene, resolves to give their brother a proper burial. Soon, a nervous sentry arrives at the palace to tell Creon that, while the sentries slept, someone gave Polynices burial rites. Creon says that he thinks some of the dissidents of the city bribed the sentry to perform the rites, and he vows to execute the sentry if no other suspect is found.

The sentry soon exonerates himself by catching Antigone in the act of attempting to rebury her brother, the sentries having disinterred him. Antigone freely confesses her act to Creon and says that he himself defies the will of the gods by refusing Polynices burial. Creon condemns both Antigone and Ismene to death. Haemon, Creon's son and Antigone's betrothed, enters the stage. Creon asks him his opinion on the issue. Haemon seems at first to side with his father, but gradually admits his opposition to Creon's stubbornness and petty vindictiveness. Creon curses him and threatens to slay Antigone before his very eyes. Haemon storms out. Creon decides to pardon Ismene, but vows to kill Antigone by walling her up alive in a tomb.

The blind prophet Tiresias arrives, and Creon promises to take whatever advice he gives. Tiresias advises that Creon allow Polynices to be buried, but Creon refuses. Tiresias predicts that the gods will bring down curses upon the city. The words of Tiresias strike fear into the hearts of Creon and the people of Thebes, and Creon reluctantly goes to free Antigone from the tomb where she has been imprisoned. But his change of heart comes too late. A messenger enters and recounts the tragic events: Creon and his entourage first gave proper burial to Polynices, then heard what sounded like Haemon's voice wailing from Antigone's tomb. They went in and saw Antigone hanging from a noose, and Haemon raving. Creon's son then took a sword and thrust it at his father. Missing, he turned the sword against himself and died embracing Antigone's body. Creon's wife, Eurydice, hears this terrible news and rushes away into the palace. Creon enters, carrying Haemon's body and wailing against his own tyranny, which he knows has caused his son's death. The messenger tells Creon that he has another reason to grieve: Eurydice has stabbed herself, and, as she died, she called down curses on her husband for the misery his pride had caused. Creon kneels and prays that he, too, might die. His guards lead him back into the palace.

OEDIPUS THE KING

A plague has stricken Thebes. The citizens gather outside the palace of their king, Oedipus, asking him to take action. Oedipus replies that he already sent his brother-in-law, Creon, to the oracle at Delphi to learn how to help the city. Creon returns with a message from the oracle: the plague will end when the murderer of Laius, former king of Thebes, is caught and expelled; the murderer is within the city. Oedipus questions Creon about the murder of Laius, who was killed by thieves on his way to consult an oracle. Only one of his fellow travelers escaped alive. Oedipus promises to solve the mystery of Laius's death, vowing to curse and drive out the murderer.

Oedipus sends for Tiresias, the blind prophet, and asks him what he knows about the murder. Tiresias responds cryptically, lamenting his ability to see the truth when the truth brings nothing but pain. At first he refuses to tell Oedipus what he knows. Oedipus curses and insults the old man, going so far as to accuse him of the murder. These taunts provoke Tiresias into revealing that Oedipus himself is the murderer. Oedipus naturally refuses to believe Tiresias's accusation. He accuses Creon and Tiresias of conspiring against his life, and charges Tiresias with insanity. He asks why Tiresias did nothing when Thebes suffered under a plague once before. At that time, a Sphinx held the city captive and refused to leave until someone answered her riddle. Oedipus brags that he alone was able to solve the puzzle. Tiresias defends his skills as a prophet, noting that Oedipus's parents found him trustworthy. At this mention of his parents, Oedipus, who grew up in the distant city of Corinth, asks how Tiresias knew his parents. But Tiresias answers enigmatically. Then, before leaving the stage, Tiresias puts forth one last riddle, saying that the murderer of Laius will turn out to be both father and brother to his own children, and the son of his own wife.

After Tiresias leaves, Oedipus threatens Creon with death or exile for conspiring with the prophet. Oedipus's wife, Jocasta (also the widow of King Laius), enters and asks why the men shout at one another. Oedipus explains to Jocasta that the prophet has charged him with Laius's murder, and Jocasta replies that all prophecies are false. As proof, she notes that the Delphic oracle once told Laius he would be murdered by his son, when in fact his son was cast out of Thebes as a baby, and Laius was murdered by a band of thieves. Her description of Laius's murder, however, sounds familiar to Oedipus, and he asks further questions. Jocasta tells him that Laius was killed at a three-way crossroads, just before Oedipus arrived in Thebes. Oedipus, stunned, tells his wife that he may be the one who murdered Laius. He tells Jocasta that, long ago, when he was the prince of Corinth, he overheard someone mention at a banquet that he was not really the son of the king and queen. He therefore traveled to the oracle of Delphi, who did not answer him but did tell him he would murder his father and sleep with his mother. Hearing this, Oedipus fled his home, never to return. It was then, on the journey that would take him to Thebes, that Oedipus was confronted and harassed by a group of travelers, whom he killed in self-defense. This skirmish occurred at the very crossroads where Laius was killed.

Oedipus sends for the man who survived the attack, a shepherd, in the hope that he will not be identified as the murderer. Outside the palace, a messenger approaches Jocasta and tells her that he has come from Corinth to inform Oedipus that his father, Polybus, is dead, and that Corinth has asked Oedipus to come and rule there in his place. Jocasta rejoices, convinced that Polybus's death from natural causes has disproved the prophecy that Oedipus would murder his father. At Jocasta's summons, Oedipus comes outside, hears the news, and rejoices with her. He now feels much more inclined to agree with the queen in deeming prophecies worthless and viewing chance as the principle governing the world. But while Oedipus finds great comfort in the fact that one-half of the prophecy has been disproved, he still fears the other half—the half that claimed he would sleep with his mother.

The messenger remarks that Oedipus need not worry, because Polybus and his wife, Merope, are not Oedipus's biological parents. The messenger, a shepherd by profession, knows firsthand that Oedipus came to Corinth as an orphan. One day long ago, he was tending his sheep when another shepherd approached him carrying a baby, its ankles pinned together. The messenger took the baby to the royal family of Corinth, and they raised him as their own. That baby was Oedipus. Oedipus asks who the other shepherd was, and the messenger answers that he was a servant of Laius.

Oedipus asks that this shepherd be brought forth to testify, but Jocasta, beginning to suspect the truth, begs her husband not to seek more information. She runs back into the palace. The shepherd then enters. Oedipus interrogates him, asking who gave him the baby. The shepherd refuses to disclose anything, and Oedipus threatens him with torture. Finally, he answers that the child came from the house of Laius. Questioned further, he answers that the baby was in fact the child of Laius himself, and that it was Jocasta who gave him the infant, ordering him to kill it, as it had been prophesied that the child would kill his parents. But the shepherd pitied the child, and decided that the prophecy could be avoided just as well if the child were to grow up in a foreign city, far from his true parents. The shepherd therefore passed the boy on to the shepherd in Corinth.

Realizing who he is and who his parents are, Oedipus screams that he sees the truth and flees back into the palace. The shepherd and the messenger slowly exit the stage. A second messenger enters and describes scenes of suffering. Jocasta has hanged herself, and Oedipus, finding her dead, has pulled the pins from her robe and stabbed out his own eyes. Oedipus now emerges from the palace, bleeding and begging to be exiled. He asks Creon to send him away from Thebes and to look after his daughters, Antigone and Ismene. Creon, covetous of royal power, is all too happy to oblige.

OEDIPUS AT COLONUS

After years of wandering in exile from Thebes, Oedipus arrives in a grove outside Athens. Blind and frail, he walks with the help of his daughter, Antigone. Oedipus and Antigone learn from a citizen that they are standing on holy ground, reserved for the Eumenides, goddesses of fate. Oedipus sends the citizen to fetch Theseus, the king of Athens and its surroundings. Oedipus tells Antigone that, earlier in his life, when Apollo prophesied his doom, the god promised Oedipus that he would come to rest on this ground.

After an interlude in which Oedipus tells the Chorus who he is, Oedipus's second daughter, Ismene, enters, having gone to learn news from Apollo's oracle at Delphi. She tells him that, back in

Thebes, Oedipus's younger son, Eteocles, has overthrown Poly-nices, the elder, and that Polynices is now amassing troops in Argos for an attack on his brother and on Creon, who rules along with Eteocles. The oracle has predicted that the burial place of Oedipus will bring good fortune to the city in which it is located, and both sons, as well as Creon, know of this prophecy. Both Polynices and Creon are currently en route to try to take Oedipus into custody and thus claim the right to bury him in their kingdoms. Oedipus swears he will never give his support to either of his sons, for they did noth-ing to prevent his exile years ago.

King Theseus arrives and says that he pities Oedipus for the fate that has befallen him, and he asks how he can help Oedipus. Oedipus asks Theseus to harbor him in Athens until his death, but warns that by doing him this favor, Theseus will incur the wrath of Thebes. Despite the warning, Theseus agrees to help Oedipus.

Creon appears in order to abduct Oedipus, but, proving unsuc-cessful, he kidnaps Antigone and Ismene instead. Theseus promises Oedipus that he will get his daughters back. Theseus does in fact return with Oedipus's daughters shortly.

Soon after, Polynices arrives, seeking his father's favor in order to gain custody of his eventual burial site. Oedipus asks Theseus to drive Polynices away, but Antigone convinces her father to listen to his son. Polynices tells Oedipus that he never condoned his exile, and that Eteocles is the bad son, having bribed the men of Thebes to turn against Polynices. Oedipus responds with a terrible curse, up-braiding his son for letting him be sent into exile, and predicting that Eteocles and Polynices will die at one another's hands. Polynices, realizing he will never win his father's support, turns to his sisters. He asks that they provide him with a proper burial should he die in battle. Antigone embraces Polynices, saying that he is condemning himself to death, but he resolutely says that his life remains in the hands of the gods. He prays for the safety of his sisters and then leaves for Thebes.

Terrible thunder sounds, and the Chorus cries out in horror. Oedipus says that his time of death has come. Sending for Theseus, he tells the king he must carry out certain rites on his body, and that by doing so he may assure divine protection to his city. Theseus says that he believes Oedipus and asks what to do. Oedipus answers that he will lead the king to the place where he will die, and that Theseus must never reveal that spot, but pass it on to his son at his own death, who in turn must pass it on to his own son. In this way

Theseus and his heirs may always rule over a safe city. Oedipus then strides off with a sudden strength, taking his daughters and Theseus to his grave.

A messenger enters to narrate the mysterious death of Oedipus: his death seemed a disappearance of sorts, "the lightless depths of Earth bursting open in kindness to receive him" (1886–1887). Just as the messenger finishes his story, Antigone and Ismene come onstage, chanting a dirge. Antigone wails that they will cry for Oedipus for as long as they live. Not knowing where to go now, Antigone says they will have to wander forever alone. Theseus returns to the stage, asking the daughters to stop their weeping. They plead to see their father's tomb, but Theseus insists that Oedipus has forbidden it. They give up their pleas but ask for safe passage back to Thebes, so that they may prevent a war between their brothers. Theseus grants them this, and the Chorus tells the girls to stop their weeping, for all rests in the hands of the gods. Theseus and the Chorus exit toward Athens; Antigone and Ismene head for Thebes.

CHARACTER LIST

Oedipus The protagonist of *Oedipus the King* and *Oedipus at Colonus*. Oedipus becomes king of Thebes before the action of *Oedipus the King* begins. He is renowned for his intelligence and his ability to solve riddles—he saved the city of Thebes and was made its king by solving the riddle of the Sphinx, the supernatural being that had held the city captive. Yet Oedipus is stubbornly blind to the truth about himself. His name's literal meaning ("swollen foot") is the clue to his identity—he was taken from the house of Laius as a baby and left in the mountains with his feet bound together. On his way to Thebes, he killed his biological father, not knowing who he was, and proceeded to marry Jocasta, his biological mother.

Jocasta Oedipus's wife and mother, and Creon's sister. Jocasta appears only in the final scenes of *Oedipus the King*. In her first words, she attempts to make peace between Oedipus and Creon, pleading with Oedipus not to banish Creon. She is comforting to her husband and calmly tries to urge him to reject Tiresias's terrifying prophecies as false. Jocasta solves the riddle of Oedipus's identity before Oedipus does, and she expresses her love for her son and husband in her desire to protect him from this knowledge.

Antigone Child of Oedipus and Jocasta, and therefore both Oedipus's daughter and his sister. Antigone appears briefly at the end of *Oedipus the King,* when she says goodbye to her father as Creon prepares to banish Oedipus. She appears at greater length in *Oedipus at Colonus,* leading and caring for her old, blind father in his exile. But Antigone comes into her own in *Antigone.* As that play's protagonist, she demonstrates a courage and clarity of sight unparalleled by any other character in the three Theban plays. Whereas other characters—Oedipus, Creon, Polynices—are reluctant to acknowledge the consequences of their actions, Antigone is unabashed in her conviction that she has done right.

Creon   Oedipus's brother-in-law, Creon appears more than any other character in the three plays combined. In him more than anyone else we see the gradual rise and fall of one man's power. Early in *Oedipus the King,* Creon claims to have no desire for kingship. Yet, when he has the opportunity to grasp power at the end of that play, Creon seems quite eager. We learn in *Oedipus at Colonus* that he is willing to fight with his nephews for this power, and in *Antigone* Creon rules Thebes with a stubborn blindness that is similar to Oedipus's rule. But Creon never has our sympathy in the way Oedipus does, because he is bossy and bureaucratic, intent on asserting his own authority.

Polynices   Son of Oedipus, and thus also his brother. Polynices appears only very briefly in *Oedipus at Colonus.* He arrives at Colonus seeking his father's blessing in his battle with his brother, Eteocles, for power in Thebes. Polynices tries to point out the similarity between his own situation and that of Oedipus, but his words seem opportunistic rather than filial, a fact that Oedipus points out.

Tiresias   Tiresias, the blind soothsayer of Thebes, appears in both *Oedipus the King* and *Antigone.* In *Oedipus the King,* Tiresias tells Oedipus that he is the murderer he hunts, and Oedipus does not believe him. In *Antigone,* Tiresias tells Creon that Creon himself is bringing disaster upon Thebes, and Creon does not believe him. Yet, both Oedipus and Creon claim to trust Tiresias deeply. The literal blindness of the soothsayer points to the metaphorical blindness of those who refuse to believe the truth about themselves when they hear it spoken.

Haemon	Creon's son, who appears only in *Antigone*. Haemon is engaged to marry Antigone. Motivated by his love for her, he argues with Creon about the latter's decision to punish her.
Ismene	Oedipus's daughter Ismene appears at the end of *Oedipus the King* and to a limited extent in *Oedipus at Colonus* and *Antigone*. Ismene's minor part underscores her sister's grandeur and courage. Ismene fears helping Antigone bury Polynices but offers to die beside Antigone when Creon sentences her to die. Antigone, however, refuses to allow her sister to be martyred for something she did not have the courage to stand up for.
Theseus	The king of Athens in *Oedipus at Colonus*. A renowned and powerful warrior, Theseus takes pity on Oedipus and defends him against Creon. Theseus is the only one who knows the spot at which Oedipus descended to the underworld—a secret he promises Oedipus he will hold forever.
Chorus	Sometimes comically obtuse or fickle, sometimes perceptive, sometimes melodramatic, the Chorus reacts to the events onstage. The Chorus's reactions can be lessons in how the audience should interpret what it is seeing, or how it should not interpret what it is seeing.
Eurydice	Creon's wife.

ANALYSIS OF MAJOR CHARACTERS

OEDIPUS

Oedipus is a man of swift action and great insight. At the opening of *Oedipus the King*, we see that these qualities make him an excellent ruler who anticipates his subjects' needs. When the citizens of Thebes beg him to do something about the plague, for example, Oedipus is one step ahead of them—he has already sent Creon to the oracle at Delphi for advice. But later, we see that Oedipus's habit of acting swiftly has a dangerous side. When he tells the story of killing the band of travelers who attempted to shove him off the three-way crossroads, Oedipus shows that he has the capacity to behave rashly.

At the beginning of *Oedipus the King,* Oedipus is hugely confident, and with good reason. He has saved Thebes from the curse of the Sphinx and become king virtually overnight. He proclaims his name proudly as though it were itself a healing charm: "Here I am myself— / you all know me, the world knows my fame: / I am Oedipus" (7–9). By the end of this tragedy, however, Oedipus's name will have become a curse, so much so that, in *Oedipus at Colonus,* the Leader of the Chorus is terrified even to hear it and cries: "You, you're that man?" (238).

Oedipus's swiftness and confidence continue to the very end of *Oedipus the King.* We see him interrogate Creon, call for Tiresias, threaten to banish Tiresias and Creon, call for the servant who escaped the attack on Laius, call for the shepherd who brought him to Corinth, rush into the palace to stab out his own eyes, and then demand to be exiled. He is constantly in motion, seemingly trying to keep pace with his fate, even as it goes well beyond his reach. In *Oedipus at Colonus,* however, Oedipus seems to have begun to accept that much of his life is out of his control. He spends most of his time sitting rather than acting. Most poignant are lines 825–960, where Oedipus gropes blindly and helplessly as Creon takes his children from him. In order to get them back, Oedipus must rely wholly on Theseus.

Once he has given his trust to Theseus, Oedipus seems ready to find peace. At Colonus, he has at last forged a bond with someone, found a kind of home after many years of exile. The single most significant action in *Oedipus at Colonus* is Oedipus's deliberate move offstage to die. The final scene of the play has the haste and drive of the beginning of *Oedipus the King,* but this haste, for Oedipus at least, is toward peace rather than horror.

ANTIGONE

Antigone is very much her father's daughter, and she begins her play with the same swift decisiveness with which Oedipus began his. Within the first fifty lines, she is planning to defy Creon's order and bury Polynices. Unlike her father, however, Antigone possesses a remarkable ability to remember the past. Whereas Oedipus defies Tiresias, the prophet who has helped him so many times, and whereas he seems almost to have forgotten his encounter with Laius at the three-way crossroads, Antigone begins her play by talking about the many griefs that her father handed down to his children. Because of her acute awareness of her own history, Antigone is much more dangerous than Oedipus, especially to Creon. Aware of the kind of fate her family has been allotted, Antigone feels she has nothing to lose. The thought of death at Creon's hands that so terrifies Ismene does not even faze Antigone, who looks forward to the glory of dying for her brother. Yet even in her expression of this noble sentiment, we see the way in which Antigone continues to be haunted by the perversion that has destroyed her family. Speaking about being killed for burying Polynices, she says that she will lie with the one she loves, loved by him, and it is difficult not to hear at least the hint of sexual overtones, as though the self-destructive impulses of the Oedipus family always tend toward the incestuous.

Antigone draws attention to the difference between divine law and human law. More than any other character in the three plays, she casts serious doubt on Creon's authority. When she points out that his edicts cannot override the will of the gods or the unshakable traditions of men, she places Creon's edict against Polynices' burial in a perspective that makes it seem shameful and ridiculous. Creon sees her words as merely a passionate, wild outburst, but he will ultimately be swayed by the words of Tiresias, which echo those of Antigone. It is important to note, however, that Antigone's motivation for burying Polynices is more complicated than simply reverence for the dead or for tradition. She says that she would never have taken upon herself the responsibility of defying the edict for the sake of a husband or children, for husbands and children can be replaced; brothers, once the parents are dead, cannot. In *Antigone* we see a woman so in need of familial connection that she is desperate to maintain the connections she has even in death.

CREON

Creon spends more time onstage in these three plays than any other character except the Chorus. His presence is so constant and his words so crucial to many parts of the plays that he cannot be dismissed as simply the bureaucratic fool he sometimes seems to be. Rather, he represents the very real power of human law and of the human need for an orderly, stable society. When we first see Creon in *Oedipus the King*, Creon is shown to be separate from the citizens of Thebes. He tells Oedipus that he has brought news from the oracle and suggests that Oedipus hear it inside. Creon has the secretive, businesslike air of a politician, which stands in sharp contrast to Oedipus, who tells him to speak out in front of everybody. While Oedipus insists on hearing Creon's news in public and builds his power as a political leader by espousing a rhetoric of openness, Creon is a master of manipulation. While Oedipus is intent on saying what he means and on hearing the truth—even when Jocasta begs and pleads with him not to—Creon is happy to dissemble and equivocate.

At lines 651–690, Creon argues that he has no desire to usurp Oedipus as king because he, Jocasta, and Oedipus rule the kingdom with equal power—Oedipus is merely the king in name. This argument may seem convincing, partly because at this moment in the play we are disposed to be sympathetic toward Creon, since Oedipus has just ordered Creon's banishment. In response to Oedipus's hotheaded foolishness, Creon sounds like the voice of reason. Only in the final scene of *Oedipus the King*, when Creon's short lines demonstrate his eagerness to exile Oedipus and separate him from his children, do we see that the title of king is what Creon desires above all.

Creon is at his most dissembling in *Oedipus at Colonus*, where he once again needs something from Oedipus. His honey-tongued speeches to Oedipus and Theseus are made all the more ugly by his cowardly attempt to kidnap Antigone and Ismene. In *Antigone*, we at last see Creon comfortable in the place of power. Eteocles and Polynices, like their father, are dead, and Creon holds the same unquestioned supremacy that Oedipus once held. Of course, once Creon achieves the stability and power that he sought and Oedipus possessed, he begins to echo Oedipus's mistakes. Creon denounces Tiresias, for example (1144–1180), obviously echoing Oedipus's denunciation in *Oedipus the King* (366–507). And, of course, Creon's penitent wailings in the final lines of *Antigone* echo those of Oedipus at the end of *Oedipus the King*. What can perhaps most be said most in favor of Creon is that in his final lines he also begins to sound like Antigone, waiting for whatever new disaster fate will bring him. He cries out that he is "nothing," "no one," but it is his suffering that makes him seem human in the end.

THE CHORUS

The Chorus reacts to events as they happen, generally in a predictable, though not consistent, way. It generally expresses a longing for calm and stability. For example, in *Oedipus the King,* it asks Oedipus not to banish Creon (725–733); fearing a curse, it attempts to send Oedipus out of Colonus in *Oedipus at Colonus* (242–251); and it questions the wisdom of Antigone's actions in *Antigone* (909–962). In moments like these, the Chorus seeks to maintain the status quo, which is generally seen to be the wrong thing. The Chorus is not cowardly so much as nervous and complacent—above all, it hopes to prevent upheaval.

The Chorus is given the last word in each of the three Theban plays, and perhaps the best way of understanding the different ways in which the Chorus can work is to look at each of these three speeches briefly. At the end of *Oedipus the King,* the Chorus conflates the people of "Thebes" with the audience in the theater. The message of the play, delivered directly to that audience, is one of complete despair: "count no man happy till he dies, free of pain at last" (1684). Because the Chorus, and not one of the individual characters, delivers this message, the play ends by giving the audience a false sense of closure. That is, the Chorus makes it sound like Oedipus is dead, and their final line suggests there might be some relief. But the audience must immediately realize, of course, that Oedipus is not dead. He wanders, blind and miserable, somewhere outside of Thebes. The audience, like Oedipus, does not know what the future holds in store. The play's ability to universalize, to make the audience feel implicated in the emotions of the Chorus as well as those of the protagonist, is what makes it a particularly harrowing tragedy, an archetypal story in Western culture.

The Chorus at the end of *Oedipus at Colonus* seems genuinely to express the thought that there is nothing left to say, because everything rests in the hands of the gods. As with Oedipus's death, the Chorus expresses no great struggle here, only a willing resignation that makes the play seem hopeful—if ambivalently so—rather than despairing. Oedipus's wandering has, it seems, done some good. The final chorus of *Antigone,* on the other hand, seems on the surface much more hopeful than either of the other two but is actually much more ominous and ambivalent. *Antigone* ends with a hope for knowledge—specifically the knowledge that comes out of suffering. This ending is quite different from the endings of the other two plays, from a mere truism about death or the fact that fate lies outside human control. The audience can agree with and believe in a statement like "Wisdom is by far the greatest part of joy," and perhaps feel that Creon has learned from his suffering, like Antigone seemingly did at the beginning of the play.

While the Chorus may believe that people learn through suffering, Sophocles may have felt differently. *Antigone* represents the last events in a series begun by *Oedipus the King,* but it was written before either of the other two Oedipus plays. And in the two subsequent plays, we see very little evidence in *Antigone* that suffering teaches anyone anything except how to perpetuate it.

THEMES, MOTIFS & SYMBOLS

THEMES

Themes are the fundamental and often universal ideas explored in a literary work.

THE POWER OF UNWRITTEN LAW

After defeating Polynices and taking the throne of Thebes, Creon commands that Polynices be left to rot unburied, his flesh eaten by dogs and birds, creating an "obscenity" for everyone to see (*Antigone*, 231). Creon thinks that he is justified in his treatment of Polynices because the latter was a traitor, an enemy of the state, and the security of the state makes all of human life—including family life and religion—possible. Therefore, to Creon's way of thinking, the good of the state comes before all other duties and values. However, the subsequent events of the play demonstrate that some duties are more fundamental than the state and its laws. The duty to bury the dead is part of what it means to be human, not part of what it means to be a citizen. That is why Polynices' rotting body is an "obscenity" rather than a crime. Moral duties—such as the duties owed to the dead—make up the body of unwritten law and tradition, the law to which Antigone appeals.

THE WILLINGNESS TO IGNORE THE TRUTH

When Oedipus and Jocasta begin to get close to the truth about Laius's murder, in *Oedipus the King*, Oedipus fastens onto a detail in the hope of exonerating himself. Jocasta says that she was told that Laius was killed by "strangers," whereas Oedipus knows that he acted alone when he killed a man in similar circumstances. This is an extraordinary moment because it calls into question the entire truth-seeking process Oedipus believes himself to be undertaking. Both Oedipus and Jocasta act as though the servant's story, once spoken, is irrefutable history. Neither can face the possibility of what it would mean if the servant were wrong. This is perhaps why Jocasta feels she can tell Oedipus of the prophecy that her son would kill his father, and Oedipus can tell her about the similar prophecy given him by an oracle (867–875), and neither feels compelled to remark on the coincidence; or why Oedipus can hear the story of Jocasta binding her child's ankles (780–781) and not think of his own swollen feet. While the information in these speeches is largely intended to make the audience painfully aware of the tragic irony, it also emphasizes just how desperately Oedipus and Jocasta do not want to speak the obvious truth: they look at the circumstances and details of everyday life and pretend not to see them.

THE LIMITS OF FREE WILL

Prophecy is a central part of *Oedipus the King*. The play begins with Creon's return from the oracle at Delphi, where he has learned that the plague will be lifted if Thebes banishes the man who killed Laius. Tiresias prophesies the capture of one who is both father and brother to his own children. Oedipus tells Jocasta of a prophecy he heard as a youth, that he would kill his father and sleep with his mother, and Jocasta tells Oedipus of a similar prophecy given to Laius, that her son would grow up to kill his father. Oedipus and Jocasta debate the extent to which prophecies should be trusted at all, and when all of the prophecies come true, it appears that one of Sophocles' aims is to justify the powers of the gods and prophets, which had recently come under attack in fifth-century B.C. Athens.

Sophocles' audience would, of course, have known the story of Oedipus, which only increases the sense of complete inevitability about how the play would end. It is difficult to say how justly one can accuse Oedipus of being "blind" or foolish when he seems to have no choice about fulfilling the prophecy: he is sent away from Thebes as a baby and by a remarkable coincidence saved and raised as a prince in Corinth. Hearing that he is fated to kill his father, he flees Corinth and, by a still more remarkable coincidence, ends up back in Thebes, now king and husband in his actual father's place. Oedipus seems only to desire to flee his fate, but his fate continually catches up with him. Many people have tried to argue that Oedipus brings about his catastrophe because of a "tragic flaw," but nobody has managed to create a consensus about what Oedipus's flaw actually is. Perhaps his story is meant to show that error and disaster can happen to anyone, that human beings are relatively powerless before fate or the gods, and that a cautious humility is the best attitude toward life.

MOTIFS

> *Motifs are recurring structures, contrasts, and literary devices
> that can help to develop and inform the text's major themes.*

SUICIDE

Almost every character who dies in the three Theban plays does
so at his or her own hand (or own will, as is the case in *Oedipus at
Colonus*). Jocasta hangs herself in *Oedipus the King* and Antigone
hangs herself in *Antigone*. Eurydice and Haemon stab themselves at
the end of *Antigone*. Oedipus inflicts horrible violence on himself
at the end of his first play, and willingly goes to his own mysterious
death at the end of his second. Polynices and Eteocles die in battle
with one another, and it could be argued that Polynices' death at
least is self-inflicted in that he has heard his father's curse and knows
that his cause is doomed. Incest motivates or indirectly brings about
all of the deaths in these plays.

SIGHT AND BLINDNESS

References to eyesight and vision, both literal and metaphorical, are
very frequent in all three of the Theban plays. Quite often, the image
of clear vision is used as a metaphor for knowledge and insight. In
fact, this metaphor is so much a part of the Greek way of thinking
that it is almost not a metaphor at all, just as in modern English:
to say "I see the truth" or "I see the way things are" is a perfectly
ordinary use of language. However, the references to eyesight and
insight in these plays form a meaningful pattern in combination
with the references to literal and metaphorical blindness. Oedipus
is famed for his clear-sightedness and quick comprehension, but he
discovers that he has been blind to the truth for many years, and
then he blinds himself so as not to have to look on his own chil-
dren/siblings. Creon is prone to a similar blindness to the truth in
Antigone. Though blind, the aging Oedipus finally acquires a limited prophetic vision. Tiresias is blind, yet he sees farther than others.
Overall, the plays seem to say that human beings can demonstrate
remarkable powers of intellectual penetration and insight, and that
they have a great capacity for knowledge, but that even the smartest
human being is liable to error, that the human capability for knowledge is ultimately quite limited and unreliable.

GRAVES AND TOMBS

The plots of *Antigone* and *Oedipus at Colonus* both revolve around burials, and beliefs about burial are important in *Oedipus the King* as well. Polynices is kept above ground after his death, denied a grave, and his rotting body offends the gods, his relatives, and ancient traditions. Antigone is entombed alive, to the horror of everyone who watches. At the end of *Oedipus the King*, Oedipus cannot remain in Thebes or be buried within its territory, because his very person is polluted and offensive to the sight of gods and men. Nevertheless, his choice, in *Oedipus at Colonus,* to be buried at Colonus confers a great and mystical gift on all of Athens, promising that nation victory over future attackers. In Ancient Greece, traitors and people who murder their own relatives could not be buried within their city's territory, but their relatives still had an obligation to bury them. As one of the basic, inescapable duties that people owe their relatives, burials represent the obligations that come from kinship, as well as the conflicts that can arise between one's duty to family and to the city-state.

SYMBOLS

Symbols are objects, characters, figures, and colors used to represent abstract ideas or concepts.

OEDIPUS'S SWOLLEN FOOT

Oedipus gets his name, as the Corinthian messenger tells us in *Oedipus the King,* from the fact that he was left in the mountains with his ankles pinned together. Jocasta explains that Laius abandoned him in this state on a barren mountain shortly after he was born. The injury leaves Oedipus with a vivid scar for the rest of his life. Oedipus's injury symbolizes the way in which fate has marked him and set him apart. It also symbolizes the way his movements have been confined and constrained since birth, by Apollo's prophecy to Laius.

THE THREE-WAY CROSSROADS

In *Oedipus the King,* Jocasta says that Laius was slain at a place where three roads meet. This crossroads is referred to a number of times during the play, and it symbolizes the crucial moment, long before the events of the play, when Oedipus began to fulfill the dreadful prophecy that he would murder his father and marry his mother. A crossroads is a place where a choice has to be made, so

THE OEDIPUS PLAYS ❀ 25

crossroads usually symbolize moments where decisions will have important consequences but where different choices are still possible. In *Oedipus the King,* the crossroads is part of the distant past, dimly remembered, and Oedipus was not aware at the time that he was making a fateful decision. In this play, the crossroads symbolizes fate and the awesome power of prophecy rather than freedom and choice.

ANTIGONE'S ENTOMBMENT

Creon condemns Antigone to a horrifying fate: being walled alive inside a tomb. He intends to leave her with just enough food so that neither he nor the citizens of Thebes will have her blood on their hands when she finally dies. Her imprisonment in a tomb symbolizes the fact that her loyalties and feelings lie with the dead—her brothers and her father—rather than with the living, such as Haemon or Ismene. But her imprisonment is also a symbol of Creon's lack of judgment and his affronts to the gods. Tiresias points out that Creon commits a horrible sin by lodging a living human being inside a grave, as he keeps a rotting body in daylight. Creon's actions against Antigone and against Polynices' body show him attempting to invert the order of nature, defying the gods by asserting his own control over their territories.

Summary & Analysis

Antigone, Lines 1–416

My own flesh and blood—dear sister, dear Ismene,
how many griefs our father Oedipus handed down!

(See QUOTATIONS, p. 57)

Summary

Night has fallen in Thebes. The preceding days have borne witness to the armed struggle between Eteocles and Polynices, sons of Oedipus and brothers to Antigone and Ismene. The brothers, who were fighting for control of Thebes, have now died at each other's hands. Polynices' invading army has retreated, and Creon now rules the city. Antigone approaches an altar in the palace, bemoaning the death of her brothers. Ismene follows close behind, echoing Antigone's sentiments.

Antigone laments Creon's recent decree that whoever tries to bury or mourn Polynices must be put to death. Although Ismene declares that the sisters lack any power in the situation, Antigone insists that she will bury Polynices, and asks for Ismene's help. Ismene contends that though she loves Polynices, she must follow the king's decree—she does not want to risk punishment by death. Antigone rejects Ismene's arguments, saying that she holds honor and love higher than law and death. Antigone exits, still resolved to bury Polynices. Ismene declares that she will always love Antigone, and then withdraws into the palace.

The Chorus, composed of the elders of Thebes, comes forward. It sings an ode praising the glory of Thebes and denouncing the proud Polynices, who nearly brought the city to ruin. Creon then enters, assuring the citizens that order and safety have returned to Thebes. He announces that Eteocles, who defended Thebes, will receive a hero's burial, unlike his brother, who shall rot in godless shame for having raised arms against the city. The Chorus says that it will obey Creon's edict.

A sentry enters with a message for the king, but he hesitates to speak for fear of the king's reaction. Creon orders him to tell his story, and he finally reports the scandalous news. Someone has given proper burial rites to Polynices' corpse, and no one knows who has done it. Unsure what to do, the sentries assigned to keep watch over the grave finally resolve to tell the king. The Chorus suggests that the gods themselves may have undertaken Polynices' burial, but Creon denounces this notion as absurd, arguing that the gods would never side with a traitor. He himself theorizes that dissidents in the city have bribed one of the sentries to defy his edict, and he accuses the present sentry of the crime. Refusing to listen to the sentry's desperate denials, Creon threatens the sentry with death if no other suspect is found, and then enters the palace. The sentry declares his intention to leave Thebes forever, and flees.

The Chorus sings an ode about how man dominates the earth and how only death can master him. But it warns that man should use his powers only in accordance with the laws of the land and the justice of the gods; society cannot tolerate those who exert their will to reckless ends.

ANALYSIS

The opening events of the play quickly establish the central conflict. Creon has decreed that the traitor Polynices must not be given proper burial, and Antigone is the only one who will speak against this decree and insist on the sacredness of family. Whereas Antigone sees no validity in a law that disregards the duty family members owe one another, Creon's point of view is exactly opposite. He has no use for anyone who places private ties above the common good, as he proclaims firmly to the Chorus and the audience as he revels in his victory over Polynices. Creon's first speech, which is dominated by words such as "principle," "law," "policy," and "decree," shows the extent to which Creon fixates on government and law as the supreme authority. Between Antigone and Creon there can be no compromise—they both find absolute validity in the respective loyalties they uphold.

In the struggle between Creon and Antigone, Sophocles' audience would have recognized a genuine conflict of duties and values. In their ethical philosophy, the ancient Athenians clearly recognized that conflicts can arise between two separate but valid principles, and that such situations call for practical judgment and deliberation. From the Greek point of view, both Creon's and Antigone's positions are flawed, because both oversimplify ethical life by recognizing only one kind of "good" or duty. By oversimplifying, each ignores the fact that a conflict exists at all, or that deliberation is necessary. Moreover, both Creon and Antigone display the dangerous flaw of pride in the way they justify and carry out their decisions. Antigone admits right from the beginning that she wants to carry out the burial because the action is "glorious." Creon's pride is that of a tyrant. He is inflexible and unyielding, unwilling throughout the play to listen to advice. The danger of pride is that it leads both these characters to overlook their own human finitude—the limitations of their own powers.

Oddly enough, the comical, lower-class messenger is the only character to exhibit the uncertainty and careful weighing of alternatives required by practical judgment. The sentry has no fixed idea of an appropriate course of action. He says that as he was coming to deliver his message, he was lost in thought, turning back and forth, pondering the consequences of what he might say and do. The sentry's comic wavering seems, at this point, like the only sensible way of acting in this society: unlike Creon or Antigone or even Ismene, the sentry considers the possible alternatives to his present situation. As a comic character, the sentry offsets the brutal force of Creon's will. Whereas the conflict between Creon and Antigone is a violent clash of two opposing, forceful wills, Creon's injustice is clearest when he promises to kill the sentry if the person responsible for Polynices' burial is not found.

The two times the Chorus speaks in this section, it seems to side with Creon and the established power of Thebes. The Chorus's first speech (117–179) describes the thwarted pride of the invading enemy: Zeus hates bravado and bragging. Yet this paean to the victory of Thebes through the graces of Zeus has a subtly critical edge. The Chorus's focus on pride and the fall of the prideful comments underhandedly on the willfulness we have just seen in Antigone and will see in Creon. Few speeches in the Oedipus plays are more swollen with self-importance than Creon's first speech, where he assumes the "awesome task of setting the city's course" and reiterates his decree against the traitor Polynices (199).

The second choral ode begins on an optimistic note but becomes darker toward the end. This ode celebrates the "wonder" of man, but the Greek word for wonderful (*deinon*) has already been used twice in the play with the connotation of "horrible" or "frightening" (the messenger and Chorus use it to describe the mysterious burial of the body). The Chorus seems to praise man for being able to accomplish whatever goal he sets his sights on—crossing the sea in winter, snaring birds and beasts, taming wild horses. But the point of the ode is that while man may be able to *master* nature by developing techniques to achieve his goals, man should formulate those goals by taking into consideration the "mood and mind for law," justice, and the common good. Otherwise, man becomes a monster.

In his first speech, Creon also uses imagery of mastery to describe the way he governs—he holds the "ship of state" on course (180). The logical problem with Creon's rhetoric is that maintaining the ship cannot be the ultimate good or goal in life, as he seems to think. Ships travel with some further end in mind, not for the sake of traveling. Similarly, the stability of the state may be important, but only because that stability enables the pursuit of other human goals, such as honoring family, gods, and loved ones.

Antigone, lines 417–700

Summary

The Chorus sees the sentry who had resolved never to return approaching, now escorting Antigone. The sentry tells the Chorus that Antigone is the culprit in the illegal burial of Polynices and calls for Creon. When Creon enters, the sentry tells him that after he and the other sentries dug up the rotting body, a sudden dust storm blinded them. When the storm passed, they saw Antigone, who cursed them and began to bury the body again. The sentries seized her and interrogated her, and she denied nothing. When Creon asks her himself, Antigone again freely admits her culpability. Creon dismisses the sentry and asks Antigone if she knew of his edict forbidding her brother's burial. Antigone declares that she knew the edict but argues that in breaking it she defied neither the gods nor justice, only the decree of an unjust man.

The Leader of the Chorus likens Antigone's passionate wildness to her father's. Creon, calling for the guards to bring Ismene, condemns both sisters to death. Antigone tells Creon that his moralizing speeches repel her, and that to die for having buried her brother honorably will bring her great glory. She tells him that all of Thebes supports her but fears to speak out against the king. Creon asks Antigone if she didn't consider Polynices' burial an insult to her other brother, Eteocles, for the two fought as enemies. Antigone insists that both deserved proper burials, regardless of their political affiliations. She says that her nature compels her to act according to love and not to bear grudges. Creon rebuffs her, saying he will never allow a woman to tell him what to do.

Ismene emerges from the palace, weeping, and says that she will share the guilt with her sister. Antigone refuses to let her do this, arguing that she acted alone and insulting Ismene for her cowardice. Creon declares both sisters mad, and again condemns them to death. Ismene attempts to save Antigone by appealing to Creon's love for his son, Haemon, who is betrothed to Antigone. But Creon stands firm, as the idea of seeing his son married to a traitor repulses him. Creon orders his guards to bind the sisters and take them away.

The Chorus sings an ode lamenting the fortunes of the house of Oedipus, which once again stands mired in death and sorrow. The Chorus prays to Zeus, guardian of kinship ties, whose law prevails above all others.

ANALYSIS

Antigone and Creon's direct confrontation further clarifies the nature of their disagreement. Antigone attacks Creon's edicts on the grounds that his interpretation of justice and the will of Zeus is invalid. She may be correct in her assessment, but in saying so she assumes the power to independently interpret justice and the will of the gods, just as Creon did. Her accusations are wild and reckless, and she seems to be trying to seize glory like the bravados the chorus condemned in their first ode.

Nevertheless, our sympathies are most likely tipping toward Antigone in this encounter. Just before the argument between Antigone and Creon, the sentry gives a vivid and disgusting description of the disinterment of Polynices' corpse. Polynices' rotting body is the physical evidence, or perhaps a symbol, of the injustice of Creon's decree and of the ruin it will bring about in Thebes. The description of the degradation of the corpse prepares the audience to be sympathetic to Antigone's arguments, even as she flies in the face of law with a pride that easily matches Creon's. Antigone draws a distinction between divine law and human law, between the "great unwritten, unshakable traditions" and the edicts of individual rulers such as Creon (502–503).

When Creon responds to Antigone's recklessness, he speaks of breaking and taming her (528–548). His words echo those of the second choral ode. Although, according to the Chorus, breaking and taming is what humans do to nature, it's not clear that Creon is "weav[ing] in / the laws of the land and the justice of the god" into his goal of breaking Antigone, as the second choral ode dictates must occur. Blood ties seem to mean nothing to Creon, who commits sacrilege against Zeus when he dismisses his blood tie to Antigone by saying that he would reject his entire family if they were huddled together at Zeus's altar. He insists he would punish Antigone even if she were a closer blood relative (543–545), and he quite arbitrarily decides at that point to punish Ismene as well. Creon's rage at Antigone's "insolence" (536) entirely consumes him, and he acts with a rashness terrifying to all who have heard him claim to hold steady control of the "ship of state."

Creon's anger is notably directed toward the fact that he is being challenged by women. When he first meets with Antigone, he says that if she gets away with her actions, she will be "the man" rather than him (541). And after he has condemned the sisters to death, he tells his guards to keep them from running loose and tie them up, so that they will act like women (652–653). In Creon's view, Antigone has overstepped the bounds of her positions as a citizen and as a human being. Antigone, of course, has none of these worldly concerns. She is prepared to die for what she believes is the right action in the eyes of the gods.

The third choral ode is more pessimistic than those before it. The Chorus takes Antigone's trespass and capture as an occasion to lament the misfortunes of Oedipus's house. It goes on (famously) to conclude that once ruin strikes a family, it continues ceaselessly through generations—no person has the power to reverse the pattern of misery and devastation. Power, the Chorus tells us, really belongs in hands of the gods, of Zeus. This third ode clarifies the second by showing that for all his seeming marvels and wonders, man is not actually powerful at all, as the disastrous fate of Oedipus's family shows. The ode concludes with the warning that when disaster strikes, it may be in the form of a "fraud" that steals on one slowly. A human being can wander into a situation in which he's wrong about everything, courting disaster. The admonishing nature of this ode seems to be subtly directed toward Creon, although we may only pick up on this in hindsight.

ANTIGONE, LINES 701–1090

Better to fall from power, if fall we must,
at the hands of a man—never be rated
inferior to a woman, never.

(See QUOTATIONS, p. 58)

SUMMARY

The Chorus sees Creon's son Haemon approaching and wonders what he thinks of Antigone's arrest. When Creon questions him about his loyalties, Haemon replies that no woman is as important as his father and that he will obey Creon. Pleased, the king praises his son's wisdom. Haemon reports that he has heard it said among the people that Antigone does not deserve such punishment for her noble-seeming deed. He implores his father not to be so sure of his rightness. Insulted by the idea that his citizens should tell him how to rule, Creon vigorously defends his absolute authority, and Haemon responds that Creon is stubborn and proud. Creon, enraged, reels off insults at his son, calling him disrespectful and the slave of a woman. Haemon responds forcefully, and even darkly hints that Creon's murder of Antigone may cause the death of another person. Creon calls for Antigone to be brought out and murdered in front of her groom, but Haemon exclaims that his father will see him no longer and rushes off. Once his son is gone, Creon concedes that he will not kill Ismene, but he promises a living death for Antigone: he will enclose her, alive, in a tomb.

Creon goes back into the palace, and the Chorus sings of the power of love, which cannot be defeated by arms, and which can drive a sane man mad. When Antigone approaches, the Chorus announces that even it would rebel upon seeing the pitiful girl being led from the palace to her tomb. Antigone tells the elders her death will be noble, but the Chorus doubts her, regarding her nobility as pride. Antigone raves when the Chorus compares her to her father, and she cries out against the fortunes of herself and her family. Creon comes out of the palace, insists that Antigone is protesting too much, and tells the guards to take her to her tomb. Before leaving, Antigone gives one last defense: she would not have defied Creon if the unburied corpse were her husband's or her child's, for either could be replaced. Only for a sibling whose parents are dead, the last son of the terrible house of Oedipus, is she willing to accept such punishment. As she is taken away, she cries out that Thebes is ruled by cowards who punish her for revering the gods. Antigone is taken to her tomb, and the Chorus sings an ode describing the mythological figures who have shared Antigone's fate, walled alive in tombs.

ANALYSIS

The Chorus and Creon both anticipate that Haemon will resist his father's decree, because they both know the power of eros, or erotic love, a topic introduced in this section. We can infer from Haemon's rage, his hints at suicide, and from the Chorus's ode on love that Haemon is indeed in the grip of passion. Even so, Haemon's arguments with Creon are rational. He says that reason is a gift of the gods, and he cautions Creon against being single-minded and self-involved, noting that there is no such thing as a one-man city. He asserts that everyone has to give way somewhat, listen, and change, and that no one is infallible. The Leader of the Chorus advises them to listen to each other, but Creon, although he as much as admits that he's a tyrant, refuses to be lectured. Haemon's and the Chorus's arguments against Creon's tyranny would have appealed to the democratic spirit of Sophocles' Athenian audience.

Given the play's themes so far, one would not necessarily expect the chorus to say that love is what has caused the play's strife. The Love Ode implies that perhaps neither Haemon nor Creon is really motivated by practical reason or right judgment, and that one or both is in the grip of blind passion. The chorus develops its earlier theme that humans should be humble, characterizing love as a force that is more powerful than "wondrous" man. Later, in the ode that describes Danae and other mythological figures, the Chorus describes people who have been sealed up in tombs while still alive. It uses what happened to these characters as a metaphor for fate, which traps all of us, in the sense that we aren't in control of our destinies.

It might be argued that love is one of the greater goods that the state exists to enable people to pursue—one of the greater goods that Creon overlooks when he argues that the well-being of the state is the highest good in human life. Creon argues that since Haemon's will should be subject to his, Haemon should not experience any conflict of loyalties. He goes on to contend that Haemon shouldn't even be attracted to Antigone if she is an enemy of the state. As he has throughout the play, Creon denies that ethical conflicts can arise, or that ethical decisions sometimes require deliberation. He insists upon remaining consistent with the views he has already stated, and asserts that he will not make himself a liar. Again, he commits sacrilege, dismissively referring to her hymns to Zeus.

Antigone's final speech is very strange. She says that she would not have suffered her ordeal for a husband but will suffer it for her brother because he is not replaceable. Yet we must remember that she is martyring herself for a dead brother, not, as she suggests, for a live one. Her final, puzzling speech may suggest that her value judgments have become distorted.

ANTIGONE, LINES 1091–1470

SUMMARY

A boy leads in Tiresias, the blind soothsayer of Thebes. Creon swears that he will obey whatever advice Tiresias gives him, since he owes so much to his past advice. Tiresias tells him that his refusal to bury Polynices and his punishment of Antigone for the burial will bring the curses of the gods down on Thebes. Hearing this, Creon curses Tiresias, calling him a false prophet who traffics in poor advice and rhetoric. Creon accuses all prophets of being power-hungry fools, but Tiresias turns the insult back on tyrants like Creon. The old prophet argues that the rites for the dead are the concern of the gods—mortals can rule only in this world. Unwilling to hear any more abuse, Tiresias has his boy lead him away. The Chorus is terrified by Tiresias's prophecy. Creon admits that he too is worried and will do whatever the citizens recommend. They call for him to free Antigone, and he reluctantly leaves to do so. Once he is gone, the Chorus prays to Dionysus to protect Thebes.

A messenger enters and tells the Chorus that a catastrophic event has taken place offstage: Haemon is dead by his own hand. As the messenger is leaving, Eurydice, Creon's wife, enters from the palace. She has overheard the commotion caused by the messenger's announcement and asks the messenger to tell her what has happened. He reports that just as Creon and his entourage had finished their burial of Polynices, they heard what sounded like Haemon's voice wailing from Antigone's tomb. They went in and saw Antigone hanging from a noose and Haemon raving. Creon's son then took a sword and thrust it at his father. Missing, he turned the sword against himself, and died embracing Antigone's body.

Hearing that Haemon is dead, Eurydice rushes back into the palace, followed by the messenger. Creon then enters, carrying Haemon's body and wailing against his own tyranny, which caused his son's death. Just then the messenger emerges and tells the king that the queen has committed suicide, brought to unbearable misery by her son's death. Creon weeps and raves wildly as Eurydice's body is brought forth from the palace. The messenger tells Creon that Eurydice called down curses on her husband for the misery his pride had caused just before she stabbed herself. Creon kneels and prays for death. His guards lead him back into the palace. The Chorus sings a final ode about how the proud are brought low by the gods.

ANALYSIS

Throughout the play, Creon has emphasized the importance of "healthy" practical judgment over a sick, twisted mind, but Tiresias informs Creon that practical judgment is precisely what he lacks— only Creon has a sick and twisted mind. When the catastrophes occur, the messenger directly points to the moral that the worst ill afflicting mortals is a lack of judgment (1373). We may well wonder what use judgment is given the limitations of human beings and the inescapable will of the gods. Perhaps the best explanation is that possessing wisdom and judgment means acknowledging human limitations and behaving piously so as not to actually call down the gods' wrath. Humans must take a humble, reverential attitude toward fate, the gods, and the limits of human intelligence. At the end of the play, Creon shows he has learned this lesson at last when, instead of mocking death as he has throughout the play, he speaks respectfully of "death" heaping blows upon him (1413–1419).

Even though Antigone exhibits a blamable pride and a hunger for glory, her transgressions are less serious than those of Creon. Antigone's crime harms no one directly, whereas Creon's mistakes affect an entire city. We learn from Tiresias that new armies are rising up in anger against Thebes because of Creon's treatment of their dead (1201–1205). More important, Creon's refusal to bury Polynices represents a more radical affront to human values than Antigone's refusal to heed Creon's edict. Creon says at the beginning of the play that the sight of Polynices' unburied corpse is an obscenity (231), but he clearly doesn't understand the implications of his own words. Whereas Antigone breaks a law made by a particular ruler in a particular instance, a law that he could have made differently, Creon violates an unwritten law, a cultural custom.

The Chorus's final speech is a remarkably terse list of possible lessons that can be learned from the play's events: wisdom is good, reverence for the gods is necessary, pride is bad, and fate is inevitable

(1466–1470). The Chorus claims that the punishing blows of fate will teach men wisdom, but it is hard to feel convinced by their words: Creon's "wisdom"—his understanding of his crimes—seems, much like Oedipus's, only to have brought him more pain. And Haemon, Antigone, and Eurydice can learn nothing more, now that they are dead. The Chorus, like the audience, struggles to find purpose in violence, though it is not clear that there is any purpose to be found.

OEDIPUS THE KING, LINES 1–337

SUMMARY

Oedipus steps out of the royal palace of Thebes and is greeted by a procession of priests, who are in turn surrounded by the impoverished and sorrowful citizens of Thebes. The citizens carry branches wrapped in wool, which they offer to the gods as gifts. Thebes has been struck by a plague, the citizens are dying, and no one knows how to put an end to it. Oedipus asks a priest why the citizens have gathered around the palace. The priest responds that the city is dying and asks the king to save Thebes. Oedipus replies that he sees and understands the terrible fate of Thebes, and that no one is more sorrowful than he. He has sent Creon, his brother-in-law and fellow ruler, to the Delphic oracle to find out how to stop the plague. Just then, Creon arrives, and Oedipus asks what the oracle has said. Creon asks Oedipus if he wants to hear the news in private, but Oedipus insists that all the citizens hear. Creon then tells what he has learned from the god Apollo, who spoke through the oracle: the murderer of Laius, who ruled Thebes before Oedipus, is in Thebes. He must be driven out in order for the plague to end.

Creon goes on to tell the story of Laius's murder. On their way to consult an oracle, Laius and all but one of his fellow travelers were killed by thieves. Oedipus asks why the Thebans made no attempt to find the murderers, and Creon reminds him that Thebes was then more concerned with the curse of the Sphinx. Hearing this, Oedipus resolves to solve the mystery of Laius's murder.

The Chorus enters, calling on the gods Apollo, Athena, and Artemis to save Thebes. Apparently, it has not heard Creon's news about Laius's murderer. It bemoans the state of Thebes, and finally invokes Dionysus, whose mother was a Theban. Oedipus returns and tells the Chorus that he will end the plague himself. He asks if anyone knows who killed Laius, promising that the informant will be rewarded and the murderer will receive no harsher punishment than exile. No one responds, and Oedipus furiously curses Laius's murderer and anyone who is protecting him. Oedipus curses himself, proclaiming that should he discover the murderer to be a member of his own family, that person should be struck by the same exile and harsh treatment that he has just wished on the murderer. Oedipus castigates the citizens of Thebes for letting the murderer go unknown so long. The Leader of the Chorus suggests that Oedipus call for Tiresias, a great prophet, and Oedipus responds that he has already done so.

ANALYSIS

Oedipus is notable for his compassion, his sense of justice, his swiftness of thought and action, and his candor. At this early stage in the play, Oedipus represents all that an Athenian audience—or indeed any audience—could desire in a citizen or a leader. In his first speech, which he delivers to an old priest whose suffering he seeks to alleviate, he continually voices his concern for the health and well-being of his people. He insists upon allowing all his people to hear what the oracle has said, despite Creon's suggestion that Oedipus hear the news in private. When Creon retells the story of Laius's murder, Oedipus is shocked and dismayed that the investigation of the murder of a king was so swiftly dropped (145–147). Oedipus quickly hatches plans to deal with both his people's suffering and Laius's unsolved murder, and he has even anticipated the Chorus's suggestions that he send someone to the oracle and call forth Tiresias. Finally, Oedipus is vehement in his promises of dire punishment for Laius's murderer, even if the murderer turns out to be someone close to Oedipus himself.

Sophocles' audience knew the ancient story of Oedipus well, and would therefore interpret the greatness Oedipus exudes in the first scene as a tragic harbinger of his fall. Sophocles seizes every opportunity to exploit this dramatic irony. Oedipus frequently alludes to sight and blindness, creating many moments of dramatic irony, since the audience knows that it is Oedipus's metaphorical blindness to the relationship between his past and his present situation that brings about his ruin. For example, when the old priest tells Oedipus that the people of Thebes are dying of the plague, Oedipus says that he could not fail to *see* this (68–72). Oedipus eagerly attempts to uncover the truth, acting decisively and scrupulously refusing to shield himself from the truth. Although we are able to see him as a mere puppet of fate, at some points, the irony is so magnified that it seems almost as if Oedipus brings catastrophe upon himself willingly. One such instance of this irony is when Oedipus proclaims proudly—but, for the audience, painfully—that he possesses the bed of the former king, and that marriage might have even created "blood-bonds" between him and Laius had Laius not been murdered (294–300).

Although the Chorus's first ode (168–244) piously calls to the gods to save Thebes from the plague, the answer they get to their prayer arrives in human form. Immediately following the ode, Oedipus enters and says that he will answer the Chorus's prayers. For a moment, Oedipus takes upon himself the role of a god—a role the Chorus has been both reluctant and eager to allow him (see 39–43). Oedipus is so competent in the affairs of men that he comes close to dismissing the gods, although he does not actually blaspheme, as Creon does in *Antigone*. At this early moment, we see Oedipus's dangerous pride, which explains his willful blindness and, to a certain extent, justifies his downfall.

Oedipus the King, lines 338–706

Summary

A boy leads in the blind prophet Tiresias. Oedipus begs him to reveal who Laius's murderer is, but Tiresias answers only that he knows the truth but wishes he did not. Puzzled at first, then angry, Oedipus insists that Tiresias tell Thebes what he knows. Provoked by the anger and insults of Oedipus, Tiresias begins to hint at his knowledge. Finally, when Oedipus furiously accuses Tiresias of the murder, Tiresias tells Oedipus that Oedipus himself is the curse. Oedipus dares Tiresias to say it again, and so Tiresias calls Oedipus the murderer. The king criticizes Tiresias's powers wildly and insults his blindness, but Tiresias only responds that the insults will eventually be turned on Oedipus by all of Thebes. Driven into a fury by the accusation, Oedipus proceeds to concoct a story that Creon and Tiresias are conspiring to overthrow him.

The leader of the Chorus asks Oedipus to calm down, but Tiresias only taunts Oedipus further, saying that the king does not even know who his parents are. This statement both infuriates and intrigues Oedipus, who asks for the truth of his parentage. Tiresias answers only in riddles, saying that the murderer of Laius will turn out to be both brother and father to his children, both son and husband to his mother. The characters exit and the Chorus takes the stage, confused and unsure whom to believe. They resolve that they will not believe any of these accusations against Oedipus unless they are shown proof.

Creon enters, soon followed by Oedipus. Oedipus accuses Creon of trying to overthrow him, since it was he who recommended that Tiresias come. Creon asks Oedipus to be rational, but Oedipus says that he wants Creon murdered. Both Creon and the leader of the Chorus try to get Oedipus to understand that he's concocting fantasies, but Oedipus is resolute in his conclusions and his fury.

ANALYSIS

As in *Antigone,* the entrance of Tiresias signals a crucial turning point in the plot. But in *Oedipus the King,* Tiresias also serves an additional role—his blindness augments the dramatic irony that governs the play. Tiresias is blind but can see the truth; Oedipus has his sight but cannot. Oedipus claims that he longs to know the truth; Tiresias says that seeing the truth only brings one pain. In addition to this unspoken irony, the conversation between Tiresias and Oedipus is filled with references to sight and eyes. As Oedipus grows angrier, he taunts Tiresias for his blindness, confusing physical sight and insight, or knowledge. Tiresias matches Oedipus insult for insult, mocking Oedipus for his eyesight and for the brilliance that once allowed him to solve the riddle of the Sphinx—neither quality is now helping Oedipus to see the truth.

In this section, the characteristic swiftness of Oedipus's thought, words, and action begins to work against him. When Tiresias arrives at line 340, Oedipus praises him as an all-powerful seer who has shielded Thebes from many a plague. Only forty lines later, he refers to Tiresias as "scum," and soon after that accuses him of treason. Oedipus sizes up a situation, makes a judgment, and acts—all in an instant. While this confident expedience was laudable in the first section, it is exaggerated to a point of near absurdity in the second. Oedipus asks Tiresias and Creon a great many questions—questions are his typical mode of address and frequently a sign of his quick and intelligent mind—but they are merely rhetorical, for they accuse and presume rather than seek answers. Though Tiresias has laid the truth out plainly before Oedipus, the only way Oedipus can interpret the prophet's words is as an attack, and his quest for information only seeks to confirm what he already believes.

The Chorus seems terrified and helpless in this section, and its speech at lines 526–572 is fraught with uncertainty and anxiety. Though, like Oedipus, the Chorus cannot believe the truth of what Tiresias has said, the Chorus does not believe itself to be untouchable as Oedipus does, consisting as it does of the plague-stricken, innocent citizens of Thebes. The Chorus's speech is full of images of caves, darkness, lightning, and wings, which suggest darkness, the unknown, and, most significantly, terror striking from the skies. The Chorus's supplications to the benevolent gods of lines 168–244 are long past. The gods are still present in this speech, but they are no longer of any help, because they know truths that they will not reveal. Thebes is menaced rather than protected by the heavens.

OEDIPUS THE KING, LINES 707–1007

SUMMARY

Oedipus's wife, Jocasta, enters and convinces Oedipus that he should neither kill nor exile Creon, though the reluctant king remains convinced that Creon is guilty. Creon leaves, and the Chorus reassures Oedipus that it will always be loyal to him. Oedipus explains to Jocasta how Tiresias condemned him, and Jocasta responds that all prophets are false. As proof, she offers the fact that the Delphic oracle told Laius he would be murdered by his son, while actually his son was cast out of Thebes as a baby and Laius was murdered by a band of thieves. Her narrative of his murder, however, sounds familiar to Oedipus, and he asks to hear more.

Jocasta tells him that Laius was killed at a three-way crossroads, just before Oedipus arrived in Thebes. Oedipus, stunned, tells his wife that he may be the one who murdered Laius. He tells Jocasta that, long ago, when he was the prince of Corinth, he heard at a banquet that he was not really the son of the king and queen, and so went to the oracle of Delphi, which did not answer him but did tell him he would murder his father and sleep with his mother. Hearing this, Oedipus fled from home, never to return. It was then, on the journey that would take him to Thebes, that Oedipus was confronted and harassed by a group of travelers, whom he killed in self-defense, at the very crossroads where Laius was killed.

Hoping that he will not be identified as Laius's murderer, Oedipus sends for the shepherd who was the only man to survive the attack. Oedipus and Jocasta leave the stage, and the Chorus enters, announcing that the world is ruled by destiny and denouncing prideful men who would defy the gods. At the same time, the Chorus worries that if all the prophecies and oracles are wrong—if a proud man can, in fact, triumph—then the gods may not rule the world after all. Jocasta enters from the palace to offer a branch wrapped in wool to Apollo.

ANALYSIS

Whatever sympathy we might have lost for Oedipus amid his ranting in the second section, we regain at least partially in the third. After Jocasta intercedes in the fight between Oedipus and Creon, Oedipus calms down and recalls that there is a riddle before him that he, as the ruler of Thebes, has a responsibility to solve. Consequently, his incessant questions become more purposeful than they were in his conversations with Tiresias and Creon. We see that Oedipus logically and earnestly pursues the truth when he does not have a preconceived idea of what the truth is. When Oedipus seizes upon the detail of the three-way crossroads (805–822), he proves that he was not merely grandstanding in the first scene of the play when he expressed his desire to be forthright with his citizens and to subject himself to the same laws he imposes upon others. In his speech at lines 848–923, Oedipus shows that he truly believes he killed Laius and is willing to accept not only the responsibility but the punishment for the act. The speech is heartbreaking because we know that Oedipus has arrived at only half the truth.

In this section, Jocasta is both careless and maternal. She tells Oedipus that prophecies do not come true, and she uses the fact that an oracle incorrectly prophesied that Laius would be killed by his own son as evidence. Jocasta's mistake is similar to Oedipus's in the previous section: she confuses conclusions and evidence. As Oedipus assumed that Tiresias's unpleasant claims could only be treason, so Jocasta assumes that because one prophecy has apparently not come to pass, prophecies can only be lies. While Oedipus's hasty and imperfect logic in the second section has much to do with his pride, Jocasta's in this section seem attached to an unwitting desire to soothe and mother Oedipus. When Jocasta is not answering Oedipus's questions, she is calming him down, asking him to go into the palace, telling him that he has nothing to worry about—no need to ask more questions—for the rest of his life. Jocasta's casual attitude upsets the Chorus, which continues to be loyal to Oedipus throughout this section (see 761–767). The Chorus's ode at lines 954–997 serves as a reminder that neither Oedipus, Jocasta, nor

THE OEDIPUS PLAYS ❦ 43

the sympathetic audience should feel calm, because oracles speak to a purpose and are inspired by the gods who control the destiny of men. Throughout the play, the Chorus has been miserable, desperate for the plague to end and for stability to be restored to the city. Nevertheless, the Chorus holds staunchly to the belief that the prophesies of Tiresias will come true. For if they do not, there is no order on earth or in the heavens.

OEDIPUS THE KING, LINES 1008–1310

And as for this marriage with your mother—
have no fear. Many a man before you,
in his dreams, has shared his mother's bed.
Take such things for shadows, nothing at all—
Live, Oedipus, as if there's no tomorrow!

(See QUOTATIONS, *p. 58)*

SUMMARY

A messenger enters, looking for Oedipus. He tells Jocasta that he has come from Corinth to tell Oedipus that his father, Polybus, is dead, and that Corinth wants Oedipus to come and rule there. Jocasta rejoices, convinced that since Polybus is dead from natural causes, the prophecy that Oedipus will murder his father is false. Oedipus arrives, hears the messenger's news, and rejoices with Jocasta; king and queen concur that prophecies are worthless and the world is ruled by chance. However, Oedipus still fears the part of the prophecy that said he would sleep with his mother. The messenger says he can rid himself of that worry, because Polybus and his wife, Merope, are not really Oedipus's natural parents.

The messenger explains that he used to be a shepherd years ago. One day, he found a baby on Mount Cithaeron, near Thebes. The baby had its ankles pinned together, and the former shepherd set them free. That baby was Oedipus, who still walks with a limp because of the injury to his ankles so long ago. When Oedipus inquires who left him in the woods on the mountain, the messenger replies that another shepherd, Laius's servant, gave him baby Oedipus. At this, Jocasta turns sharply, seeming to sense some horrible revelation on the horizon.

Oedipus wants to find this shepherd, so he can find out who his natural parents are. Jocasta begs him to abandon his search immediately, but Oedipus is insistent. After screaming and pleading some more to no avail, Jocasta finally flees back into the palace. Oedipus dismisses her concerns as snobbish fears that he may be born of poor parents, and Oedipus and the Chorus rejoice at the possibility that they may soon know who his parents truly are.

The other shepherd, who turns out to be the same shepherd who witnessed Laius's murder, comes onto the stage. The messenger identifies him as the man who gave him the young Oedipus. Oedipus interrogates the new arrival, asking who gave him the baby, but the shepherd refuses to talk. Finally, after Oedipus threatens him with torture, the shepherd answers that the baby came from the house of Laius. Questioned further, he answers that it was Laius's child, and that Jocasta gave it to him to destroy because of a prophecy that the child would kill his parents. But instead, the shepherd gave him to the other shepherd, so that he might be raised as a prince in Corinth. Realizing who he is and who his parents are, Oedipus screams that he sees the truth, and flees back into the palace. The shepherd and the messenger slowly exit the stage.

Analysis

Sophocles makes the scene in which Oedipus and Jocasta learn that Polybus is dead seem strangely comic. Oedipus digests the news of Polybus's death without showing the slightest sign of grief. The moment becomes, in fact, an occasion for near triumph, as Oedipus believes his doubts about prophecies have been confirmed. He is now convinced that prophecies are useless. He even says, "Polybus / packs [all the prophecies] off to sleep with him in hell!" (1062–1063). Oedipus's strange glee reveals the extent to which he has withdrawn into himself after obtaining the knowledge that he killed his father. He and Jocasta rejoice in the smallest and most bizarre details in order to alleviate some of the guilt Oedipus feels (for another example, see Oedipus and Jocasta's discussion at lines 938–951).

Oedipus's own tenacity, however, means that he will not allow his understanding to remain incomplete. When he learns that there is still a piece of the puzzle left unsolved—the identity of the man from whom the messenger received the baby Oedipus—Oedipus seems irresistibly driven to ask questions until the whole truth is out. Thus, he gradually deprives himself of ambiguous details that could alleviate his guilt. Jocasta, of course, solves the riddle before Oedipus—she realizes she is his mother while he is still imagining himself to be the child of slaves. Oedipus must realize that something is amiss when Jocasta leaves the stage screaming, but his speech at lines 1183–1194 is strangely joyful. Chance, he says in this speech, is his mother, and the waxing and waning moon his brothers. Overwhelmed by an onslaught of new information, Oedipus re-envisions his earthly relationships as celestial ones as he announces his intent to uncover his true identity. It seems that he is unable to face directly the reality of his origins—reconceiving his identity allows him to feel a sense of control over it, but it also keeps that identity ambiguous. He basically identifies himself as someone who must search for his identity. Oedipus, who is famous for his skill at solving riddles, thus makes his own life into a riddle.

The messenger and shepherd are both similar to and different from the messenger characters who enter at the end of Greek tragedies to announce the terrible events that have occurred offstage (as will happen at the end of *Oedipus the King* [lines 1365–1422]). Like the typical final-scene messenger, these characters bear important news that is largely concerned with events that have not happened onstage. But unlike the typical final-scene messenger, these characters bear news not only to the audience but also to the man whom the news directly affects.

Because Oedipus receives news of his own tragedy, his drastic actions near the play's conclusion become an exaggerated model of how the audience is expected to react to the words of the messenger characters, who narrate the catastrophes in the final scenes of Greek plays. Throughout the play, Oedipus has been concerned with precise words—of the oracle (102), of Jocasta when she mentions the three-way crossroads (805), of the messenger who escaped death in Laius's traveling party (932–937). After learning the truth of his origins, however, Oedipus gives words physical consequence. He transforms the messenger's statement into a tangible, life-changing, physical horror, in a manner that shows the audience what its reaction should be.

OEDIPUS THE KING, LINES 1311–1684

SUMMARY

The Chorus enters and cries that even Oedipus, greatest of men, was brought low by destiny, for he unknowingly murdered his father and married his mother. The messenger enters again to tell the Chorus what has happened in the palace. Jocasta is dead, by suicide. She locked herself in her bedroom, crying for Laius and weeping for her monstrous fate. Oedipus came to the door in a fury, asking for a sword and cursing Jocasta. He finally hurled himself at the bedroom door and burst through it, where he saw Jocasta hanging from a noose. Seeing this, Oedipus sobbed and embraced Jocasta. He then took the gold pins that held her robes and, with them, stabbed out his eyes. He kept raking the pins down his eyes, crying that he could not bear to see the world now that he had learned the truth.

Just as the messenger finishes the story, Oedipus emerges from the palace. With blood streaming from his blind eyes, he fumes and rants at his fate, and at the infinite darkness that embraces him. He claims that though Apollo ordained his destiny, it was he alone who pierced his own eyes. He asks that he be banished from Thebes. The Chorus shrinks away from Oedipus as he curses his birth, his marriage, his life, and in turn all births, marriages, and lives.

Creon enters, and the Chorus expresses hope that he can restore order. Creon forgives Oedipus for his past accusations of treason and asks that Oedipus be sent inside so that the public display of shame might stop. Creon agrees to exile Oedipus from the city, but tells him that he will only do so if every detail is approved by the gods. Oedipus embraces the hope of exile, since he believes that, for some reason, the gods want to keep him alive. He says that his two sons are men and can take care of themselves, but asks that Creon take care of his girls, whom he would like to see one final time.

The girls, Antigone and Ismene, come forth, crying. Oedipus embraces them and says he weeps for them, since they will be excluded from society, and no man will want to marry the offspring of an incestuous marriage. He turns to Creon and asks him to promise that he will take care of them. He reaches out to Creon, but Creon will not touch his hand. Oedipus asks his daughters to pray that they may have a better life than his. Creon then puts an end to the farewell, saying that Oedipus has wept shamefully long enough. Creon orders the guards to take Antigone and Ismene away from Oedipus, and tells Oedipus that his power has ended. Everyone exits, and the Chorus comes onstage once more. Oedipus, greatest of men, has fallen, they say, and so all life is miserable, and only death can bring peace.

ANALYSIS

The speech of the Chorus, with which this section begins (1311–1350), turns the images of the plowman and ship's captain, which formerly stood for Oedipus's success and ability to manage the state, into images of his failure. And the way in which it does so is quite extreme, focusing particularly on the sexual aspect of Oedipus's actions. Oedipus and his father have, like two ships in one port, shared the same "wide harbor," and Oedipus has plowed the same "furrows" his father plowed (1334–1339). The harbor image ostensibly refers to Jocasta's bedchamber, but both images also quite obviously refer to the other space Oedipus and his father have shared: Jocasta's vagina.

Images of earth and soil continue throughout the scene, most noticeably in one of Oedipus's final speeches, in which he talks to his children about what he has done (see 1621–1661). These images of earth, soil, and plowing are used to suggest the metaphor of the sturdy plowman tilling the soil of the state, but they also suggest the image of the soil drinking the blood of the family members Oedipus has killed (see in particular 1531–1537). Oedipus's crimes are presented as a kind of blight on the land, a plague—symbolized by the plague with which the play begins—that infects the earth on which Oedipus, his family, and his citizens stand, and in which all are buried as a result of Oedipus's violence.

After we learn of Oedipus's self-inflicted blinding, Oedipus enters, led by a boy (1432)—a clear visual echo of the Tiresias's entrance at line 337. Oedipus has become like the blind prophet whose words he scorned. Unable to see physically, he is now possessed of an insight, or an inner sight, that is all too piercing and revealing. Though the Chorus is fascinated with the amount of physical pain Oedipus must be in after performing such an act, Oedipus makes no mention of physical pain. Like Tiresias, he has left the concerns of the physical world behind to focus on the psychological torment that accompanies contemplation of the truth.

Once the mystery of Laius's murder has been solved, Creon quickly transfers the power to himself. Even in his newfound humbleness, Oedipus still clings to some trappings of leadership, the most pathetic example being his command to Creon to bury Jocasta as he sees fit. Oedipus finds it difficult to leave the role of commander, which is why he tries to preempt Creon's power by asking Creon to banish him. Creon, however, knows that Oedipus no longer has any real control. Creon is brusque and just as efficient a leader as Oedipus was at the beginning of the play. Just as Oedipus anticipated the Chorus's demand for a consultation with the oracle in the first scene, so Creon has anticipated Oedipus's request for banishment now: when Oedipus requests banishment, Creon says that he's already consulted "the god" about it (1574). Creon has also anticipated Oedipus's desire to see his daughters, and has them brought onstage and taken away again.

Mostly because he is contrasted with Creon, Oedipus becomes a tragic figure rather than a monster in the play's final moments. Though throughout the play Oedipus has behaved willfully and proudly, he has also been earnest and forthright in all of his actions. We trust Oedipus's judgment because he always seems to mean what he says and to try to do what he believes is right. His punishment of blindness and exile seems just, therefore, because he inflicted it upon himself. Creon, on the other hand, has the outward trappings of Oedipus's candid, frank nature, but none of its substance. "I try to say what I mean; it's my habit," Creon tells Oedipus in the play's final lines, but the audience perceives this to be untrue (1671). Creon's earlier protestations that he lacked the desire for power are proved completely false by his eagerness to take Oedipus's place as king, and by the cutting ferocity with which he silences Oedipus at the end of the play. At the end of the play, one kind of pride has merely replaced another, and all men, as the Chorus goes on to say, are destined to be miserable.

OEDIPUS AT COLONUS, LINES 1–576

SUMMARY

After years of wandering in exile from Thebes, Oedipus arrives in a grove outside Athens. Blind and frail, he walks with the help of his daughter Antigone. Neither she nor Oedipus knows the place where they have come to rest, but they have heard they are on the outskirts of Athens, and the grove in which they sit bears the marks of holy ground. A citizen of Colonus approaches and insists that the ground is forbidden to mortals and that Oedipus and Antigone must leave. Oedipus inquires which gods preside over the grove and learns that the reigning gods are the Eumenides, or the goddesses of fate. In response to this news, Oedipus claims that he must not move, and he sends the citizen to fetch Theseus, the king of Athens and its environs. Oedipus then tells Antigone that, earlier in his life, when Apollo's oracle prophesied his doom, the god declared that Oedipus would die on this ground.

The Chorus enters, cursing the strangers who would dare set foot on the holy ground of Colonus. The Chorus convinces Antigone and Oedipus to move to an outcropping of rock at the side of the grove, and then interrogates Oedipus about his origins. When Oedipus reluctantly identifies himself, the Chorus cries out in horror, begging Oedipus to leave Colonus at once. Oedipus argues that he was not responsible for his horrible acts, and says that the city may benefit greatly if it does not drive him away. Oedipus expresses his arguments with such force that the Chorus fills with awe and agrees to await Theseus's pronouncement on the matter.

The next person to enter the grove is not Theseus but Ismene, Oedipus's second daughter. Oedipus and the two girls embrace. Oedipus thanks Ismene for having journeyed to gather news from the oracles, while her sister has stayed with him as his guide. Ismene bears terrible news: back in their home of Thebes, Eteocles, the younger son of Oedipus, has overthrown Polynices, his elder son. Polynices now amasses troops in Argos for an attack upon his brother and Creon, who is ruling along with Eteocles.

The oracle has predicted that Oedipus's burial place will bring good fortune to the city in which it is located. Both sons, as well as Creon, know of this prophecy, and Creon is currently en route to Colonus to try to take Oedipus into custody and thus claim the right to bury him in his kingdom. Oedipus swears he will never give his support to either of his sons, for they did nothing to prevent his exile years ago. The Chorus tells Oedipus that he must appease the spirits whom he offended when he trespassed on the sacred ground, and Ismene says that she will go and perform the requisite libation and prayer.

ANALYSIS

Oedipus at Colonus is set many years after *Oedipus the King*, and the long-wandering Oedipus has changed his perspective on his exile. First, he has decided that he was not responsible for his fate, though at the end of the previous play Oedipus proudly claimed responsibility for his actions, blinding himself and begging for exile. Oedipus has also decided that his sons should have prevented his exile, though in *Oedipus the King* his sons never even appeared onstage. We do not yet know what to make of Oedipus's revised sentiments—he may simply be a broken man making excuses, or perhaps his many years of wandering have imbued him with a new kind of wisdom.

Although Oedipus seems to have traded his former pride and disdain for kindness, the scene that opens the play creates a puzzling contradiction. The characters are trespassing on holy ground that is described lovingly by Antigone. The trespass must be rectified with libation and with prayers, and it is. At the same time, it seems odd that a play dedicated to piety begins with trespass on holy ground. What seems clear is that this Oedipus is far more devout than he once was—when a prayer or libation is called for, he agrees to it at once. Yet, although Oedipus has his daughters perform the necessary rites, he does not really apologize for his trespass. Rather, he regards himself as someone who holds knowledge of the gods beyond that of the naïve citizens. This odd tension between piety and pride will not cease but increase as the play progresses.

What Oedipus has gained in wisdom, he has lost in enthusiasm—he is now a much less dynamic and heroic character. Perhaps the older Oedipus's lack of dramatic interest is due to the fact that all of the characters are of secondary importance in this play, which is primarily concerned with rituals and religious themes that are difficult for the modern reader to understand.

OEDIPUS AT COLONUS, LINES 577–1192

SUMMARY

The Chorus gathers around Oedipus, relentlessly denouncing his crimes and insisting that he recount his tragic life story. Oedipus reluctantly tells of killing his father and marrying his mother, both crimes that he insists he undertook unknowingly. Theseus now enters, saying that he knows Oedipus's story and pities his fate. Oedipus thanks Theseus for not making him repeat his story yet again, and tells him that his body will prove a great boon to the city. Oedipus requests that Theseus provide him with proper burial in Colonus, and Theseus agrees. Oedipus then warns him that Thebes will attack Athens for the right to his body, and Theseus asks why Oedipus doesn't return home to die, if Thebes so desires his presence. In reply, Oedipus launches into a lament on the cruelty of his exile, the fragility of the bonds of friendship and love, and the untrustworthiness of all but the eternal gods, who promise protection to the city that buries him. Theseus swears that he will protect Oedipus from the Thebans and never betray him. Theseus exits, and the Chorus comes forth to praise Colonus.

Antigone sees Creon and his guards approaching. Creon notices the family's fear and insists that he comes only to bring Oedipus home and give him rest. He tells Oedipus that his pitiful wanderings bring shame upon Thebes, but Oedipus disbelieves this statement, arguing that Creon willingly sent him away. He tells that he knows why he is being courted—for the sake of the blessing the gods have promised to the possessors of his body. Oedipus tells Creon that he has no desire to return to Thebes but only to enter into the peace of death. He tries to send Creon away, but Creon refuses to relent, and orders his guards to seize Antigone and Ismene. Although the Chorus condemns Creon, it is powerless to stop him.

Creon then threatens to seize Oedipus and carry him back to Thebes. Just as he lays his hands on Oedipus, however, Theseus enters and asks the cause of the commotion. Oedipus explains what has happened, and Theseus sends his soldiers to retrieve Antigone and Ismene. He curses Creon, saying that he has shamed Thebes with his bullying behavior, but Creon justifies his actions as recourse for the hideous crimes of Oedipus. Hearing this, Oedipus again argues that he is not responsible for his fate; the gods thrust it on him. Theseus orders his men to keep watch over Creon as he goes to find Oedipus's daughters. Creon promises that although he may find himself overpowered now, he will have his revenge once he has amassed his troops back in Thebes. All but Oedipus and the Chorus leave the stage. As he exits, Theseus promises that Oedipus will get his daughters back.

ANALYSIS

Compared to the other two Theban plays, relatively little tension or unresolved conflict exists on the surface of *Oedipus at Colonus*. The plot is straightforward: Theseus is the hero and Creon is the villain; Creon takes Oedipus's daughters, and Theseus gets them back again. With the gods finally on his side, Oedipus receives what he asks for.

We begin to perceive tension within Creon's character. He is no longer a simple rational foil for Oedipus, the villain to Oedipus's hero. Instead, he stands somewhere between the stern authority of Theseus and the limitless emotion of Oedipus, and he now emerges as a force that is both willful and subversive. When Creon is alone with Oedipus and his daughters, he has the upper hand and consequently behaves in a forceful and domineering manner, ordering Antigone and Ismene taken away and threatening to kidnap Oedipus as well. Once Theseus arrives on the scene, however, Creon realizes that he must behave more subtly. Thus, instead of commanding Theseus as he did Oedipus, in lines 1070–1094 Creon attempts to persuade Theseus that Oedipus is a blight upon Athens.

Again, the characters' actions can be viewed skeptically. Theseus's protection of Oedipus from Creon, for example, may be an act of nobility, but Theseus's motivation is probably more pragmatic—

protecting Oedipus means security for his city. Oedipus, too, may not be as helpless as he tells himself he is. It seems that the blind man's refusal to return to his home is more an act of pride then one of piety, and that his insults are the cruel taunts of an embittered man. Both his refusal and his insults lead to the abduction of his daughters by Creon. Both Creon and Oedipus seem to have motives that are more complicated than they appear on the surface.

OEDIPUS AT COLONUS, LINES 1193–1645

SUMMARY

The Chorus anticipates that a glorious battle between Colonus and Thebes will be fought in which Colonus, strong and blessed, will triumph. Theseus returns, leading Antigone and Ismene, whom Oedipus embraces. He thanks Theseus for rescuing his daughters, but Theseus demurs from describing his valiant struggle to save the girls, stating that he prefers to prove himself through actions rather than words. Yet he does report that a man has recently arrived from Argos. Theseus saw the stranger praying on the altar of Poseidon, and rumor has it that the stranger wishes to speak with Oedipus.

Oedipus pleads with Theseus to drive the stranger out of Athens, realizing that it is his son Polynices, but Theseus and Antigone convince Oedipus to hear what his son has to say. They insist that one should listen to reason rather than bear old grudges. Although Oedipus disagrees in principle, he consents to listen to Polynices if Theseus promises to protect Oedipus from possible abduction. Theseus gives Oedipus his word and exits. The Chorus gathers around Oedipus and sings that to never be born is best, but that if one must be born, a short life is preferable to a long one, for life is unbearable and only death brings peace. Polynices then enters the scene.

Polynices cries out in pity at the family's fate and swears that he regrets allowing Oedipus to be sent away from Thebes. He tells of how his brother, Eteocles, bribed the men of Thebes to turn against him, and how he now plans to regain his throne by force, sending seven armies against the seven doors of Thebes. Oedipus refuses to answer his son, but the Chorus pleads for him to speak. He responds that he wishes he had never set eyes upon Polynices, and that it is quite fitting that Polynices now suffers the same exile and sorrow to which he condemned his father. Eteocles and Polynices will each die by the other's hand, he says, for that is the curse Oedipus put on them when they exiled him from Thebes.

Polynices, realizing that he'll never win his father's support, turns to his sisters, whom he asks only for a proper burial if he is killed in battle. Antigone asks her brother to call off the war, but Polynices argues that his sense of honor prevents him from such a gesture. Antigone embraces Polynices, saying that he is condemning himself to death, but he declares that his life rests in the hands of the gods. He prays for the safety of his sisters, then departs for Thebes.

ANALYSIS

The Chorus gives what can be likened to a "summary" of the central theme of *Oedipus at Colonus*: "Not to be born is best / when all is reckoned in, but once a man has seen the light / the next best thing, by far, is to go back / where he came from" (1388–1391). Of course, to treat this statement as a Sophoclean "motto" would be overly simplistic: to do so would be to ignore the poetry of the passage—the way it ranges from the joys of ceremony to the horrors of war to the invincible strength of nature. Furthermore, within the context of a play about Oedipus, this passage is colored with irony, because, all too literally, Oedipus went "back" precisely "where he came from"—Jocasta's womb.

The clash between father and son is all we see of Polynices in the trilogy, though his name will be brandished repeatedly in the play. Our fleeting glimpse of him here suggests a man driven by honor and duty but lacking Theseus's good judgment and pragmatism—a man who, it seems, greatly resembles Oedipus before his fall. His crusade is motivated by pride and self-interest, although he is not without regard for the gods. He embraces his fate with absolute forthrightness.

Oedipus's response to his son's plight is a startling invective that reaches its height when he shouts, "You—die! Die and be damned! I spit on you! Out!" (1567). Oedipus's entire speech is so powerful and bitter that we cannot help but sympathize with the curser rather than the cursed. Broken from his years of wandering, Oedipus now abhors all worldly violence and at the same time wishes only for death. Yet, it is unclear whether or not we should approve of Oedipus's absolute condemnation of his son—it seems that the play's moral lines are too crudely drawn. In the second encounter between Oedipus and Polynices, father and son will stand absolutely opposed to each other, and we are in a position to empathize with both.

OEDIPUS AT COLONUS, LINES 1646–2001

SUMMARY

> [T]here is no room for grieving here—
> it might bring down the anger of the gods.
>
> *(See* QUOTATIONS, *p. 60)*

Terrible thunder crashes, and the Chorus cries out in horror. Oedipus declares that his time of death has come and sends for Theseus. Awed by the blackening heavens, the Chorus murmurs in confusion. When Theseus appears, Oedipus informs him that the thunder signals his death, and that Theseus must carry out certain rites to assure divine protection of his city. Oedipus will lead Theseus to the place where he will die. No one but the king shall ever know that location—upon his death, each king will pass the information on to his son. In this way, Theseus's heirs will always rule over a blessed city. Oedipus then strides off with a sudden strength, bringing his daughters and Theseus offstage, to his grave.

The Chorus comes forward to pray for peace and an honorable burial for Oedipus. A messenger then enters to tell the Chorus what has happened. Oedipus led his friend and daughters to the edge of a steep descent, and then sent Antigone and Ismene to perform his final libations. When they returned, they dressed Oedipus in linen, the proper clothing for the dead. The daughters began weeping, and Oedipus swore that his infinite love would repay all the hardship they had suffered for him. Oedipus and his daughters embraced, sobbing, until a voice called out from the skies, ordering Oedipus to proceed in his task. Oedipus made Theseus promise that he would look after his daughters. He then sent the girls away, taking Theseus with him to the place where he was meant to die. When Antigone and Ismene returned, Theseus stood shielding his eyes, and Oedipus had disappeared. Theseus then bent down to kiss the ground and pray to the gods.

Just as the messenger finishes his story, Antigone and Ismene come onstage, chanting a dirge. Antigone wails that they will cry for Oedipus for as long as they live. Not knowing where to turn, Antigone says the girls will have to wander alone forever. Theseus enters, asking the daughters to stop their weeping. They beg to see their father's tomb, but the king insists that Oedipus has forbidden it. They cease their pleas, but ask for safe passage back to Thebes so that they may prevent a war between their brothers. Theseus grants them this, and the Chorus tells the girls to desist from crying, for all events in life occur according to the will of the gods. Theseus and the Chorus exit toward Athens; Antigone and Ismene head for Thebes.

ANALYSIS

Like that of *Oedipus the King*, the central theme of *Oedipus at Colonus* is self-knowledge, but in the latter play, Oedipus's self-knowledge may be too great rather than too scant. In *Oedipus the King*, the distance between Oedipus and the audience was an ironic one—we knew the truth about Oedipus, but he didn't understand it himself. In *Oedipus at Colonus*, the Oedipus's actions are all sanctified by his divine knowledge, and Oedipus has knowledge and understanding of his own plight that the rest of the characters do not have. Throughout the Theban plays, the audience is distanced from real events, especially violent ones. Since many of the play's events are reported after they occur, in narrative, the distance between the reader and Oedipus in this final play is doubled. Not only do we not see Oedipus die, no one but Theseus does.

Again, it is not an action or object that will guard Colonus, but rather language, transmitted over time. Oedipus states that his death and body are not important to the well-being of Colonus; the secret passed from son to son will be the city's true guardian. It is puzzling, though, that Sophocles built his play around a secret that is never revealed to the audience. In *Oedipus the King*, it was the audience's superior knowledge that gave it delight and sorrow. What do we feel when such knowledge is denied to us? The moment of Oedipus's secretive death is unceremonious, marked by nothing but a few prosaic lines from the Chorus, which knows as little as we do.

A modern audience is also liable to be unexpectedly unmoved by the final speeches of Antigone and Ismene. We cannot truly share in their extreme sorrow, which feels unmotivated by the events of the play, but neither do we have any reason to disapprove of it. As with the conflict between Oedipus and Polynices, there is no single way for the audience to react to feelings outside of our own categories of feeling and thought; we can only regard them with a certain emotional and moral detachment, utterly unlike what we would feel in a tragedy. *Oedipus at Colonus* is not a tragedy but rather a text that embraces its own inscrutable secrecy.

Important Quotations
Explained

1. My own flesh and blood—dear sister, dear Ismene, how
    many griefs our father Oedipus handed down! Do you
    know one, I ask you, one grief that Zeus will not perfect
    for the two of us while we still live and breathe? There's
    nothing, no pain—our lives are pain—no private shame,
    no public disgrace, nothing I haven't seen in your grief
    and mine.   (*Antigone*, 1–8)

Antigone's first words in *Antigone*, "My own flesh and blood,"
vividly emphasize the play's concern with familial relationships.
Antigone is a play about the legacy of incest and about a sister's love
for her brother. Flesh and blood have been destined to couple un-
naturally—in sex, violence, or both—since Oedipus's rash and unwitting slaying of his father. Antigone says that griefs are "handed
down" in Oedipus's family, implicitly comparing grief to a family
heirloom.

In her first speech, Antigone seems a dangerous woman, well on
her way to going over the edge. She knows she has nothing to lose,
telling Ismene, "Do you know one, I ask you, one grief / that Zeus
will not perfect for the two of us / while we still live and breathe?"
Before we even have time to imagine what the next grief might be,
Antigone reveals it: Creon will not allow her brother Polynices to
be buried. Ismene, on the other hand, like the audience, is one step
behind. From the outset, Antigone is the only one who sees what
is really going on, the only one willing to speak up and point out
the truth.

2. Anarchy—show me a greater crime in all the earth! She,
    she destroys cities, rips up houses, breaks the ranks of
    spearmen into headlong rout. But the ones who last it
    out, the great mass of them owe their lives to discipline.
    Therefore we must defend the men who live by law, never
    let some woman triumph over us. Better to fall from power,
    if fall we must, at the hands of a man—never be rated
    inferior to a woman, never.   (*Antigone*, 751–761)

This is one of Creon's speeches to the Chorus. The word "anarchy"
(in Greek, *anarchia*) literally means "without a leader." The Greek
word is feminine and can be represented by a feminine pronoun,
which is why Creon, speaking of anarchy, says, "She, she destroys
cities, rips up houses. . . ." Because Creon uses the feminine pronoun,
he sounds as if he might be talking about Antigone, and maintaining
order is certainly connected, in his mind, with keeping women in
their place. Creon sees anarchy as the inevitable consequence when
disobedience of the law is left unpunished. For Creon, the law, on
whatever scale, must be absolute. His insistence on the gender of
the city's ruler ("the man") is significant, since masculine political
authority is opposed to uncontrolled feminine disobedience. Creon
sees this feminine disobedience as something that upsets the order
of civilization on every possible level—the political ("destroys cities"), the domestic ("rips up houses"), and the military ("breaks the
ranks of spearmen"). The only way to fight this disorder is through
discipline; therefore, says Creon, "we must defend the men who live
by law, [we must] never let some woman triumph over us" (758).

3. Fear? What should a man fear? It's all chance, chance
    rules our lives. Not a man on earth can see a day ahead,
    groping through the dark. Better to live at random, best
    we can. And as for this marriage with your mother—have
    no fear. Many a man before you, in his dreams, has shared
    his mother's bed. Take such things for shadows, nothing at
    all— Live, Oedipus, as if there's no tomorrow!
                        (*Oedipus the King*, 1068–1078)

The audience, familiar with the Oedipus story, almost does not want
to listen to these self-assured lines, spoken by Jocasta, wherein she
treats incest with a startling lightness that will come back to haunt
her. What makes these lines tragic is that Jocasta has no reason to

know that what she says is foolish, ironic, or, simply, wrong. The audience's sense of the work of "fate" in this play has almost entirely to do with the fact that the Oedipus story was an ancient myth even in fifth-century B.C. Athens. The audience's position is thus most like that of Tiresias—full of the knowledge that continues to bring it, and others, pain.

At the same time, it is important to note that at least part of the irony of the passage does depend on the play, and the audience, faulting Jocasta for her blindness. Her claim that "chance rules our lives" and that Oedipus should live "as if there's no tomorrow" seems to fly in the face of the beliefs of more or less everyone in the play, including Jocasta herself. Oedipus would not have sent Creon to the oracle if he believed events were determined randomly. Nor would he have fled Corinth after hearing the prophecy of the oracle that he would kill his mother and sleep with his father; nor would Jocasta have bound her baby's ankles and abandoned him in the mountains. Again and again this play, and the other Theban plays, returns to the fact that prophecies do come true and that the words of the gods must be obeyed. What we see in Jocasta is a willingness to believe oracles only as it suits her: the oracle prophesied that her son would kill Laius and so she abandoned her son in the mountains; when Laius was not, as she thinks, killed by his son, she claims to find the words of the oracle worthless. Now she sees Oedipus heading for some potentially horrible revelation and seeks to curb his fear by claiming that everything a person does is random.

4.   People of Thebes, my countrymen, look on Oedipus. He
     solved the famous riddle with his brilliance, he rose to
     power, a man beyond all power. Who could behold his
     greatness without envy? Now what a black sea of terror
     has overwhelmed him. Now as we keep our watch and
     wait the final day, count no man happy till he dies, free of
     pain at last.   (*Oedipus the King*, 1678–1684)

These words, spoken by the Chorus, form the conclusion of *Oedipus the King*. That Oedipus "solved the famous riddle [of the Sphinx] with his brilliance" is an indisputable fact, as is the claim that he "rose to power," to an enviable greatness. In underscoring these facts, the Chorus seems to suggest a causal link between Oedipus's rise and his fall—that is, Oedipus fell *because* he rose too high, because in his pride he inspired others to "envy." But the causal relationship is never actually established, and ultimately all the Chorus demonstrates is a progression of time: "he rose to power, a man beyond all power. / . . . / Now what a black sea of terror has overwhelmed him." These lines have a ring of hollow and terrifying truth to them, because the comfort an audience expects in a moral is absent (in essence, they say "Oedipus fell for this reason; now you know how not to fall").

5.   Stop, my children, weep no more. Here where the dark
       forces store up kindness both for living and the dead, there
       is no room for grieving here—it might bring down the
       anger of the gods.

                                    (*Oedipus at Colonus*, 1970–1974)

Theseus's short speech from the end of *Oedipus at Colonus* argues that grieving might not be a good thing—a sentiment unusual in the Theban plays. Sophocles' audience would have seen, before this speech, the most extreme consequences of excessive grief: Antigone's death, Haemon's death, Eurydice's death, Jocasta's death, Oedipus's blinding, Oedipus's self-exile. The rash actions of the grief-stricken possess both a horror and a sense of inevitability or rightness. Jocasta kills herself because she cannot go on living as both wife and mother to her son; Oedipus blinds himself in order to punish himself for his blindness to his identity; Eurydice can no longer live as the wife of the man who killed her children. Theseus's speech calls attention to the fact that the violence that arises from this grieving only leads to the perpetuation of violence.

At the end of *Oedipus at Colonus*, Antigone and Ismene beg to be allowed to see their father's tomb, to complete the process of their grieving at that spot. But Theseus insists on maintaining the secret as Oedipus wished. Unlike the other two Theban plays, death is in this play a point of rest, a point at which lamentation must stop rather than begin.

KEY FACTS

FULL TITLE
Antigone, Oedipus the King, Oedipus at Colonus

AUTHOR
Sophocles

TYPE OF WORK
Play

GENRE
Antigone and *Oedipus the King* are tragedies; *Oedipus at Colonus* is difficult to classify.

LANGUAGE
Ancient Greek

TIME AND PLACE WRITTEN
Antigone is believed to have been written around 441 B.C., *Oedipus the King* around 430 B.C., and *Oedipus at Colonus* sometime near the end of Sophocles' life in 406–405 B.C. The plays were all written and produced in Athens, Greece.

DATE OF FIRST PUBLICATION
The plays probably circulated in manuscript in fifth-century B.C. Athens and have come down to modern editors through the scribal and editorial efforts of scholars in ancient Greece, ancient Alexandria, and medieval Europe.

PUBLISHER
There is no known publisher of original or early editions. The most important modern edition of the Greek texts, prepared by A. C. Pearson, was published by Oxford University Press in 1924 and reprinted with corrections in 1928.

TONE
Tragic

TENSE
Present

SETTING (TIME)
All three plays are set in the mythical past of ancient Greece.

SETTING (PLACE)

Antigone and *Oedipus the King* are set in Thebes, *Oedipus at Colonus* in Colonus (near Athens).

PROTAGONIST

Oedipus is the protagonist of both *Oedipus the King* and *Oedipus at Colonus*. Antigone is the protagonist of *Antigone*.

MAJOR CONFLICT

Antigone's major conflict is between Creon and Antigone. Creon has declared that the body of Polynices may not be given a proper burial because he led the forces that invaded Thebes, but Antigone wishes to give her brother a proper burial nevertheless. The major conflict of *Oedipus the King* arises when Tiresias tells Oedipus that Oedipus is responsible for the plague, and Oedipus refuses to believe him. The major conflict of *Oedipus at Colonus* is between Oedipus and Creon. Creon has been told by the oracle that only Oedipus's return can bring an end to the civil strife in Thebes—Oedipus's two sons, Eteocles and Polynices, are at war over the throne. Oedipus, furious at Thebes for exiling him, has no desire to return.

RISING ACTION

The rising action of *Oedipus the King* occurs when Creon returns from the oracle with the news that the plague in Thebes will end when the murderer of Laius, the king before Oedipus, is discovered and driven out. The rising action of *Oedipus at Colonus* occurs when Creon demands that Oedipus return to Thebes and tries to force him to do so. The rising action of *Antigone* is Antigone's decision to defy Creon's orders and bury her brother.

CLIMAX

The climax of *Oedipus the King* occurs when Oedipus learns, quite contrary to his expectations, that he is the man responsible for the plague that has stricken Thebes—he is the man who killed his father and slept with his mother. The climax of *Oedipus at Colonus* happens when we hear of Oedipus's death. The climax of *Antigone* is when Creon, too late to avert tragedy, decides to pardon Antigone for defying his orders and burying her brother.

FALLING ACTION

In *Oedipus the King,* the consequences of Oedipus's learning of his identity as the man who killed his father and slept with his mother are the falling action. This discovery drives Jocasta to hang herself, Oedipus to poke out his own eyes, and Creon to banish Oedipus from Thebes. The falling action of *Oedipus at Colonus* is Oedipus's curse of Polynices. The curse is followed by the onset of a storm, which Oedipus recognizes as a signal of his imminent death. The falling action of *Antigone* occurs after Creon decides to free Antigone from her tomblike prison. Creon arrives too late and finds that Antigone has hanged herself. Haemon, Antigone's fiancé, attempts to kill Creon but ends up killing himself. Creon's wife, Eurydice, stabs herself.

THEMES

The power of unwritten law, the willingness to ignore the truth, the limits of free will

MOTIFS

Suicide, sight and blindness, graves and tombs

SYMBOLS

Oedipus's swollen foot, the three-way crossroads, Antigone's entombment

FORESHADOWING

Oedipus's name, which literally means "swollen foot," foreshadows his discovery of his own identity. Tiresias, the blind prophet, appears in both *Oedipus the King* and *Antigone* and announces what will happen to Oedipus and to Creon—only to be completely ignored by both. The truth that comes from Tiresias's blindness foreshadows the revelation that inspires Oedipus to blind himself. Oedipus's command in *Oedipus at Colonus* that no one, not even his own daughters, know where he has been buried foreshadows the problems surrounding burial in *Antigone.*

STUDY QUESTIONS

1. *Discuss the role of the sentry in Antigone. How does this minor character affect our impressions of major characters, or of the play's central conflict?*

The sentry in *Antigone* is a messenger who clearly has no desire to tell his tale. The entire seventeen lines of the sentry's opening speech, in which he must report Polynices' burial to Creon, are devoted to trying not to speak. His fearful halting demonstrates that Creon is powerful and dangerous, ready to exercise his power on the most helpless—and pointless—of victims. Creon, of course, blames the sentry for burying Polynices, and the sentry complains about the dangers of rulers who judge poorly. The sentry is free to say such things at this point, because he has nothing to lose. His forthrightness offsets the ugly cruelty of Creon's power and makes Creon seem like a petty dictator rather than a moral force to be reckoned with.

   The sentry is lucky, for shortly after vowing never to return to Creon or Thebes, he enters triumphantly with Antigone, who has been caught in the act of reburying her brother's body. Although he continues to be a comical character, with his second entrance the sentry becomes less sympathetic. He boasts incessantly about being involved in a situation he formerly wanted to avoid. Also, because he turns Antigone in, he seems more complicit with Creon's power than outside of it—even though his inaction would likely have cost him his life. In response to Creon's request for details, he launches into a long and detailed description not only of the arrest but of the reburial of the body, its physical decay, the dust storm the sentries endured, and the rites Antigone administered. The sentry seems to have become something like a police officer, fully aligned with Creon. He enables Antigone's ultimate imprisonment and demise.

2. *Examine the messenger's speech narrating the death of Jocasta and the blinding of Oedipus in* OEDIPUS THE KING. *What is the messenger's attitude toward the events he describes? What is the effect of his announcement on the audience?*

The audience does not see Jocasta commit suicide or Oedipus blind himself, because in Ancient Greek theater such violent catastrophes traditionally happen offstage. The audience hears them described by witnesses rather than seeing them firsthand. Greek tragedy left more to the imagination than modern theater does. It placed a great deal of importance on the language in which the catastrophe is described. In the case of Oedipus, the convention of keeping violence offstage is thematically appropriate. The audience is faced with the realization that it is blind, that it relies for its knowledge of events on report and hearsay, and is thus prone to error and uncertainty. Over the course of the play, the once-confident Oedipus discovers that he is in the grip of uncertainty and error himself. His self-blinding symbolizes, among other things, the blindness and doubtfulness of human life in general.

The messenger suggests that the Chorus—and, implicitly, the audience—is better off having been spared these terrible spectacles, and his words guide the audience's reaction. When the messenger describes the wrenching sobs that Oedipus delivers upon seeing Jocasta, our emotions are stirred in a different way than if we had simply witnessed the violence ourselves. The focus is on the other characters' reactions to the violent acts, and on the audience's reaction, instead of on the acts themselves.

3. *What is the difference between Oedipus's relationship with Antigone and his relationship with Ismene in* OEDIPUS AT COLONUS?

In *Oedipus at Colonus,* Oedipus is almost utterly dependent on his two daughters, Antigone and Ismene. Antigone acts as Oedipus's eyes and Ismene as his ears. When they arrive at the sacred grove at Colonus, Oedipus asks Antigone to leave him and find out if anyone lives nearby, and she says that she can see a man approaching. Oedipus cannot tell that the citizen has exited until Antigone tells him so. Antigone also first perceives the approach of the Chorus, Ismene, Creon, and Polynices, and she repeatedly helps Oedipus move around the stage. Oedipus's reliance on his daughter for her sight emphasizes both his blindness and his impotence, as well as the strength of his relationship with Antigone. Given Oedipus's faltering and lack of self-reliance in these early scenes, the messenger's description of Oedipus proceeding unaided to the spot where he dies seems miraculous.

Ismene is not nearly so close with her father, as the fact that she is not so helpful with respect to Oedipus's most terrible loss—his sight—indicates. Ismene's first lines are about her not being able to see her father and sister through her tears. Immediately thereafter, she exclaims that she can hardly bear to look at her father because of the cruel fate that he has suffered. Ismene is distracted by pity and shame in a way that Antigone is not. Nevertheless, Ismene does offer practical help to her father, and it is from her that Antigone and Oedipus learn that Creon and Polynices, separately and on the advice of the oracles, seek Oedipus's blessing and body to aid them in their battles for control of Thebes. It is also Ismene who goes to perform the rites of atonement to appease the spirits on whose ground Oedipus and Antigone trespassed at the beginning of the play.

How to Write
Literary Analysis

The Literary Essay: A Step-by-Step Guide

When you read for pleasure, your only goal is enjoyment. You might find yourself reading to get caught up in an exciting story, to learn about an interesting time or place, or just to pass time. Maybe you're looking for inspiration, guidance, or a reflection of your own life. There are as many different, valid ways of reading a book as there are books in the world.

When you read a work of literature in an English class, however, you're being asked to read in a special way: you're being asked to perform *literary analysis*. To analyze something means to break it down into smaller parts and then examine how those parts work, both individually and together. Literary analysis involves examining all the parts of a novel, play, short story, or poem—elements such as character, setting, tone, and imagery—and thinking about how the author uses those elements to create certain effects.

A literary essay isn't a book review: you're not being asked whether or not you liked a book or whether you'd recommend it to another reader. A literary essay also isn't like the kind of book report you wrote when you were younger, where your teacher wanted you to summarize the book's action. A high school- or college-level literary essay asks, "How does this piece of literature actually work?" "How does it do what it does?" and, "Why might the author have made the choices he or she did?"

The Seven Steps

No one is born knowing how to analyze literature; it's a skill you learn and a process you can master. As you gain more practice with this kind of thinking and writing, you'll be able to craft a method that works best for you. But until then, here are seven basic steps to writing a well-constructed literary essay:

1. Ask questions
2. Collect evidence
3. Construct a thesis

4. Develop and organize arguments
5. Write the introduction
6. Write the body paragraphs
7. Write the conclusion

---

1. ASK QUESTIONS

When you're assigned a literary essay in class, your teacher will often provide you with a list of writing prompts. Lucky you! Now all you have to do is choose one. Do yourself a favor and pick a topic that interests you. You'll have a much better (not to mention easier) time if you start off with something you enjoy thinking about. If you are asked to come up with a topic by yourself, though, you might start to feel a little panicked. Maybe you have too many ideas—or none at all. Don't worry. Take a deep breath and start by asking yourself these questions:

- **What struck you?** Did a particular image, line, or scene linger in your mind for a long time? If it fascinated you, chances are you can draw on it to write a fascinating essay.

- **What confused you?** Maybe you were surprised to see a character act in a certain way, or maybe you didn't understand why the book ended the way it did. Confusing moments in a work of literature are like a loose thread in a sweater: if you pull on it, you can unravel the entire thing. Ask yourself why the author chose to write about that character or scene the way he or she did and you might tap into some important insights about the work as a whole.

- **Did you notice any patterns?** Is there a phrase that the main character uses constantly or an image that repeats throughout the book? If you can figure out how that pattern weaves through the work and what the significance of that pattern is, you've almost got your entire essay mapped out.

- **Did you notice any contradictions or ironies?** Great works of literature are complex; great literary essays recognize and explain those complexities. Maybe the title (*Happy Days*) totally disagrees with the book's subject matter (hungry orphans dying in the woods). Maybe the main character acts one way around his family and a completely different way around his friends and associates. If you can find a way to explain a work's contradictory elements, you've got the seeds of a great essay.

At this point, you don't need to know exactly what you're going to say about your topic; you just need a place to begin your exploration. You can help direct your reading and brainstorming by formulating your topic as a *question,* which you'll then try to answer in your essay. The best questions invite critical debates and discussions, not just a rehashing of the summary. Remember, you're looking for something you can *prove or argue* based on evidence you find in the text. Finally, remember to keep the scope of your question in mind: is this a topic you can adequately address within the word or page limit you've been given? Conversely, is this a topic big enough to fill the required length?

GOOD QUESTIONS

> *"Are Romeo and Juliet's parents responsible for the deaths of their children?"*
>
> *"Why do pigs keep showing up in* LORD OF THE FLIES?*"*
>
> *"Are Dr. Frankenstein and his monster alike? How?"*

BAD QUESTIONS

> *"What happens to Scout in* TO KILL A MOCKINGBIRD?*"*
>
> *"What do the other characters in* JULIUS CAESAR *think about Caesar?"*
>
> *"How does Hester Prynne in* THE SCARLET LETTER *remind me of my sister?"*

---

2. COLLECT EVIDENCE

Once you know what question you want to answer, it's time to scour the book for things that will help you answer the question. Don't worry if you don't know what you want to say yet—right now you're just collecting ideas and material and letting it all percolate. Keep track of passages, symbols, images, or scenes that deal with your topic. Eventually, you'll start making connections between these examples and your thesis will emerge.

Here's a brief summary of the various parts that compose each and every work of literature. These are the elements that you will analyze in your essay, and which you will offer as evidence to support your arguments. For more on the parts of literary works, see the Glossary of Literary Terms at the end of this section.

ELEMENTS OF STORY   These are the *what*s of the work—what happens, where it happens, and to whom it happens.

- **Plot:** All of the events and actions of the work.

- **Character:** The people who act and are acted upon in a literary work. The main character of a work is known as the *protagonist.*

- **Conflict:** The central tension in the work. In most cases, the protagonist wants something, while opposing forces (antagonists) hinder the protagonist's progress.

- **Setting:** When and where the work takes place. Elements of setting include location, time period, time of day, weather, social atmosphere, and economic conditions.

- **Narrator:** The person telling the story. The narrator may straightforwardly report what happens, convey the subjective opinions and perceptions of one or more characters, or provide commentary and opinion in his or her own voice.

- **Themes:** The main idea or message of the work—usually an abstract idea about people, society, or life in general. A work may have many themes, which may be in tension with one another.

ELEMENTS OF STYLE   These are the *how*s—how the characters speak, how the story is constructed, and how language is used throughout the work.

- **Structure and organization:** How the parts of the work are assembled. Some novels are narrated in a linear, chronological fashion, while others skip around in time. Some plays follow a traditional three- or five-act structure, while others are a series of loosely connected scenes. Some authors deliberately leave gaps in their works, leaving readers to puzzle out the missing information. A work's structure and organization can tell you a lot about the kind of message it wants to convey.

- **Point of view:** The perspective from which a story is told. In *first-person point of view,* the narrator involves him or herself in the story. ("I went to the store"; "We watched in horror as the bird slammed into the window.") A first-person narrator is usually the protagonist of the work, but not always. In *third-person point of view,* the narrator does not participate in the story. A third-person narrator may closely follow a specific character, recounting that individual character's thoughts or experiences, or it may be what we call an *omniscient* narrator. Omniscient narrators see and know all: they can witness any event in any time or place and are privy to the inner thoughts and feelings of all characters. Remember that the narrator and the author are not the same thing!

- **Diction:** Word choice. Whether a character uses dry, clinical language or flowery prose with lots of exclamation points can tell you a lot about his or her attitude and personality.

- **Syntax:** Word order and sentence construction. Syntax is a crucial part of establishing an author's narrative voice. Ernest Hemingway, for example, is known for writing in very short, straightforward sentences, while James Joyce characteristically wrote in long, incredibly complicated lines.

- **Tone:** The mood or feeling of the text. Diction and syntax often contribute to the tone of a work. A novel written in short, clipped sentences that use small, simple words might feel brusque, cold, or matter-of-fact.

- **Imagery:** Language that appeals to the senses, representing things that can be seen, smelled, heard, tasted, or touched.

- **Figurative language:** Language that is not meant to be interpreted literally. The most common types of figurative language are *metaphors* and *similes,* which compare two unlike things in order to suggest a similarity between them— for example, "All the world's a stage," or "The moon is like a ball of green cheese." (Metaphors say one thing *is* another thing; similes claim that one thing is *like* another thing.)

---

3. Construct a Thesis

When you've examined all the evidence you've collected and know how you want to answer the question, it's time to write your thesis statement. A *thesis* is a claim about a work of literature that needs to be supported by evidence and arguments. The thesis statement is the heart of the literary essay, and the bulk of your paper will be spent trying to prove this claim. A good thesis will be:

- **Arguable.** "*The Great Gatsby* describes New York society in the 1920s" isn't a thesis—it's a fact.

- **Provable through textual evidence.** *"Hamlet* is a confusing but ultimately very well-written play" is a weak thesis because it offers the writer's personal opinion about the book. Yes, it's arguable, but it's not a claim that can be proved or supported with examples taken from the play itself.

- **Surprising.** "Both George and Lenny change a great deal in *Of Mice and Men*" is a weak thesis because it's obvious. A really strong thesis will argue for a reading of the text that is not immediately apparent.

- **Specific.** "Dr. Frankenstein's monster tells us a lot about the human condition" is *almost* a really great thesis statement, but it's still too vague. What does the writer mean by "a lot"? *How* does the monster tell us so much about the human condition?

GOOD THESIS STATEMENTS

Question: In *Romeo and Juliet*, which is more powerful in shaping the lovers' story: fate or foolishness?

Thesis: "Though Shakespeare defines Romeo and Juliet as 'star-crossed lovers' and images of stars and planets appear throughout the play, a closer examination of that celestial imagery reveals that the stars are merely witnesses to the characters' foolish activities and not the causes themselves."

Question: How does the bell jar function as a symbol in Sylvia Plath's *The Bell Jar*?

Thesis: "A bell jar is a bell-shaped glass that has three basic uses: to hold a specimen for observation, to contain gases, and to maintain a vacuum. The bell jar appears in each of these capacities in *The Bell Jar*, Plath's semi-autobiographical novel, and each appearance marks a different stage in Esther's mental breakdown."

Question: Would Piggy in *The Lord of the Flies* make a good island leader if he were given the chance?

Thesis: "Though the intelligent, rational, and innovative Piggy has the mental characteristics of a good leader, he ultimately lacks the social skills necessary to be an effective one. Golding emphasizes this point by giving Piggy a foil in the charismatic Jack, whose magnetic personality allows him to capture and wield power effectively, if not always wisely."

4. DEVELOP AND ORGANIZE ARGUMENTS

The reasons and examples that support your thesis will form the middle paragraphs of your essay. Since you can't really write your thesis statement until you know how you'll structure your argument, you'll probably end up working on steps 3 and 4 at the same time. There's no single method of argumentation that will work in every context. One essay prompt might ask you to compare and contrast two characters, while another asks you to trace an image through a given work of literature. These questions require different kinds of answers and therefore different kinds of arguments. Below, we'll discuss three common kinds of essay prompts and some strategies for constructing a solid, well-argued case.

TYPES OF LITERARY ESSAYS

- **Compare and contrast**

    Compare and contrast the characters of Huck and Jim in THE ADVENTURES OF HUCKLEBERRY FINN.

    Chances are you've written this kind of essay before. In an academic literary context, you'll organize your arguments the same way you would in any other class. You can either go *subject by subject* or *point by point*. In the former, you'll discuss one character first and then the second. In the latter, you'll choose several traits (attitude toward life, social status, images and metaphors associated with the character) and devote a paragraph to each. You may want to use a mix of these two approaches—for example, you may want to spend a paragraph a piece broadly sketching Huck's and Jim's personalities before transitioning into a paragraph or two that describes a few key points of comparison. This can be a highly effective strategy if you want to make a counterintuitive argument—that, despite seeming to be totally different, the two objects being compared are actually similar in a very important way (or vice versa). Remember that your essay should reveal something fresh or unexpected about the text, so think beyond the obvious parallels and differences.

- **Trace**

    Choose an image—for example, birds, knives, or eyes—and trace that image throughout MACBETH.

    Sounds pretty easy, right? All you need to do is read the play, underline every appearance of a knife in *Macbeth*, and then list them in your essay in the order they appear, right? Well, not exactly. Your teacher doesn't want a simple catalog of examples. He or she wants to see you make *connections* between those examples—that's the difference between summarizing and analyzing. In the *Macbeth* example above, think about the different contexts in which knives appear in the play and to what effect. In *Macbeth,* there are real knives and imagined knives; knives that kill and knives that simply threaten. Categorize and classify your examples to give them some order. Finally, always keep the overall effect in mind. After you choose and analyze your examples, you should come to some greater understanding about the work, as well as your chosen image, symbol, or phrase's role in developing the major themes and stylistic strategies of that work.

- **Debate**

  Is the society depicted in 1984 *good for its citizens?*

  In this kind of essay, you're being asked to debate a moral, ethical, or aesthetic issue regarding the work. You might be asked to judge a character or group of characters (*Is Caesar responsible for his own demise?*) or the work itself (*Is JANE EYRE a feminist novel?*). For this kind of essay, there are two important points to keep in mind. First, don't simply base your arguments on your personal feelings and reactions. Every literary essay expects you to read and analyze the work, so search for evidence in the text. What do characters in *1984* have to say about the government of Oceania? What images does Orwell use that might give you a hint about his attitude toward the government? As in any debate, you also need to make sure that you define all the necessary terms before you begin to argue your case. What does it mean to be a "good" society? What makes a novel "feminist"? You should define your terms right up front, in the first paragraph after your introduction.

  Second, remember that strong literary essays make contrary and surprising arguments. Try to think outside the box. In the *1984* example above, it seems like the obvious answer would be no, the totalitarian society depicted in Orwell's novel is *not* good for its citizens. But can you think of any arguments for the opposite side? Even if your final assertion is that the novel depicts a cruel, repressive, and therefore harmful society, acknowledging and responding to the counterargument will strengthen your overall case.

5. WRITE THE INTRODUCTION

Your introduction sets up the entire essay. It's where you present your topic and articulate the particular issues and questions you'll be addressing. It's also where you, as the writer, introduce yourself to your readers. A persuasive literary essay immediately establishes its writer as a knowledgeable, authoritative figure.

An introduction can vary in length depending on the overall length of the essay, but in a traditional five-paragraph essay it should be no longer than one paragraph. However long it is, your introduction needs to:

- **Provide any necessary context.** Your introduction should situate the reader and let him or her know what to expect. What book are you discussing? Which characters? What topic will you be addressing?

- **Answer the "So what?" question.** Why is this topic important, and why is your particular position on the topic noteworthy? Ideally, your introduction should pique the reader's interest by suggesting how your argument is surprising or otherwise counterintuitive. Literary essays make unexpected connections and reveal less-than-obvious truths.

- **Present your thesis.** This usually happens at or very near the end of your introduction.

- **Indicate the shape of the essay to come.** Your reader should finish reading your introduction with a good sense of the scope of your essay as well as the path you'll take toward proving your thesis. You don't need to spell out every step, but you do need to suggest the organizational pattern you'll be using.

Your introduction should not:

- **Be vague.** Beware of the two killer words in literary analysis: *interesting* and *important*. Of course the work, question, or example is interesting and important—that's why you're writing about it!

- **Open with any grandiose assertions.** Many student readers think that beginning their essays with a flamboyant statement such as, "Since the dawn of time, writers have been fascinated with the topic of free will," makes them sound important and commanding. You know what? It actually sounds pretty amateurish.

- **Wildly praise the work.** Another typical mistake student writers make is extolling the work or author. Your teacher doesn't need to be told that "Shakespeare is perhaps the greatest writer in the English language." You can mention a work's reputation in passing—by referring to *The Adventures of Huckleberry Finn* as "Mark Twain's enduring classic," for example—but don't make a point of bringing it up unless that reputation is key to your argument.

- **Go off-topic.** Keep your introduction streamlined and to the point. Don't feel the need to throw in all kinds of bells and whistles in order to impress your reader—just get to the point as quickly as you can, without skimping on any of the required steps.

---

6. WRITE THE BODY PARAGRAPHS

Once you've written your introduction, you'll take the arguments you developed in step 4 and turn them into your body paragraphs. The organization of this middle section of your essay will largely be determined by the argumentative strategy you use, but no matter how you arrange your thoughts, your body paragraphs need to do the following:

- **Begin with a strong topic sentence.** Topic sentences are like signs on a highway: they tell the reader where they are and where they're going. A good topic sentence not only alerts readers to what issue will be discussed in the following paragraph but also gives them a sense of what argument will be made *about* that issue. "Rumor and gossip play an important role in *The Crucible*" isn't a strong topic sentence because it doesn't tell us very much. "The community's constant gossiping creates an environment that allows false accusations to flourish" is a much stronger topic sentence— it not only tells us *what* the paragraph will discuss (gossip) but *how* the paragraph will discuss the topic (by showing how gossip creates a set of conditions that leads to the play's climactic action).

- **Fully and completely develop a single thought.** Don't skip around in your paragraph or try to stuff in too much material. Body paragraphs are like bricks: each individual one needs to be strong and sturdy or the entire structure will collapse. Make sure you have really proven your point before moving on to the next one.

- **Use transitions effectively.** Good literary essay writers know that each paragraph must be clearly and strongly linked to the material around it. Think of each paragraph as a response to the one that precedes it. Use transition words and phrases such as *however, similarly, on the contrary, therefore,* and *furthermore* to indicate what kind of response you're making.

---

7. WRITE THE CONCLUSION

Just as you used the introduction to ground your readers in the topic before providing your thesis, you'll use the conclusion to quickly summarize the specifics learned thus far and then hint at the broader implications of your topic. A good conclusion will:

- **Do more than simply restate the thesis.** If your thesis argued that *The Catcher in the Rye* can be read as a Christian allegory, don't simply end your essay by saying, "And that is why *The Catcher in the Rye* can be read as a Christian allegory." If you've constructed your arguments well, this kind of statement will just be redundant.

- **Synthesize the arguments, not summarize them.** Similarly, don't repeat the details of your body paragraphs in your conclusion. The reader has already read your essay, and chances are it's not so long that they've forgotten all your points by now.

- **Revisit the "So what?" question.** In your introduction, you made a case for why your topic and position are important. You should close your essay with the same sort of gesture. What do your readers know now that they didn't know before? How will that knowledge help them better appreciate or understand the work overall?

- **Move from the specific to the general.** Your essay has most likely treated a very specific element of the work—a single character, a small set of images, or a particular passage. In your conclusion, try to show how this narrow discussion has wider implications for the work overall. If your essay on *To Kill a Mockingbird* focused on the character of Boo Radley, for example, you might want to include a bit in your conclusion about how he fits into the novel's larger message about childhood, innocence, or family life.

- **Stay relevant.** Your conclusion should suggest new directions of thought, but it shouldn't be treated as an opportunity to pad your essay with all the extra, interesting ideas you came up with during your brainstorming sessions but couldn't fit into the essay proper. Don't attempt to stuff in unrelated queries or too many abstract thoughts.

- **Avoid making overblown closing statements.** A conclusion should open up your highly specific, focused discussion, but it should do so without drawing a sweeping lesson about life or human nature. Making such observations may be part of the point of reading, but it's almost always a mistake in essays, where these observations tend to sound overly dramatic or simply silly.

A+ Essay Checklist

Congratulations! If you've followed all the steps we've outlined above, you should have a solid literary essay to show for all your efforts. What if you've got your sights set on an A+? To write the kind of superlative essay that will be rewarded with a perfect grade, keep the following rubric in mind. These are the qualities that teachers expect to see in a truly A+ essay. How does yours stack up?

- ✓ Demonstrates a thorough understanding of the book
- ✓ Presents an original, compelling argument
- ✓ Thoughtfully analyzes the text's formal elements
- ✓ Uses appropriate and insightful examples
- ✓ Structures ideas in a logical and progressive order
- ✓ Demonstrates a mastery of sentence construction, transitions, grammar, spelling, and word choice

SUGGESTED ESSAY TOPICS

1. *Creon is the only character with a major role in all three of the Theban plays. Does he change over the course of the three plays? If so, how?*

2. *Although there is little or no onstage violence in the Theban plays, the characters in OEDIPUS AT COLONUS are very much concerned with war. What different things does war mean to each of the play's characters?*

3. *What importance does Antigone's gender hold in ANTIGONE? How does it shape the way other characters view her?*

4. *All three of the Theban plays are shaped by Oedipus's incestuous marriage to Jocasta. What do these plays say about incest?*

5. *In each of the three plays, the Chorus repeatedly gives us moral lessons, often condemning "pride." Are we to take the proclamations of the Chorus as absolute truth, or is the Chorus just as fallible as the other characters? Is pride really the catalyst for all the catastrophes of the plays?*

A+ Student Essay

> In *Oedipus the King,* are human beings presented as
> prisoners of fate?

Sophocles' *Oedipus the King* doesn't simply depict a man who discovers, to his horror, that he is powerless to direct his own life.
Rather, the play offers an example of how individual human beings
can find ways to assert their independence within the limits determined by their destiny. Fate certainly shapes characters' lives in the
play, but it does not determine them completely.

Prophecies consistently come true in *Oedipus the King,* which
proves that fate is a real force in the world of the play. However,
the paths humans take toward their pre-determined destinations
remain for them to choose, as do the attitudes they adopt toward
the gods' decrees. Long before the play opens, Laius and Jocasta
left their son for dead to thwart the terrible prophecy that he would
someday kill his father and marry his mother. Similarly, when Oedipus learned of his fate, he fled Corinth, assuming that the prophecy
applied to Polybus, the man he believed to be his biological father.
In *Oedipus the King,* however, when Oedipus learns that it is he who
must be cast out to save Thebes from the plague, he immediately
agrees to submit to the decree and leave the city. His decision seems
partially motivated by an intense sense of shame and horror, but
throughout the play Oedipus has demonstrated his commitment to
his people, and his choice of exile seems equally driven by his desire
to see Thebes spared. The early choices he and his parents made may
have been foolish and arrogant, but his final choice affords him a
measure of tragic dignity. Sophocles' play asserts that humans have
the freedom to determine the quality of their own characters, if not
always the outcomes of their lives.

Sophocles foregrounds the issue of human freedom by setting the
play long after the initial prophecy has been fulfilled. When the play
opens, Oedipus has been living happily with Jocasta and their four
children for many years. The people of Thebes revere him as a wise
and brave leader, a man who "lifted up [their] lives" by defeating the
Sphinx. Except for the arrival of the plague, Oedipus seems to have
a happy, prosperous life. By beginning the play here, at the height
of Oedipus's success, Sophocles not only makes Oedipus's fall more
dramatic and extreme: He also shows that the crucial issue is not

whether the prophecy will come true—it already did, long ago—but how the great Oedipus will personally handle the revelation of his crimes. Tellingly, no gods appear in *Oedipus the King,* only humans. No divine figure forces Oedipus to seek out Laius's murderer or subsequently cast himself out of Thebes. The oracle from Apollo represents the only divine influence in the play, and even then several levels of human messengers stand between the god's words and Oedipus's ears.

Perhaps most telling, Oedipus himself doesn't see himself as powerless. From the beginning, Oedipus has an overwhelming sense of his own, individual power, as indicated by his constant use of the first-person pronouns *I* and *me.* "I am the land's avenger," he claims at one point. "I came by, Oedipus the ignorant, / I stopped the Sphinx!" he exalts. Oedipus is a man of vigorous action, as demonstrated by the way he relentlessly pursues the truth, even as it becomes clear the truth may implicate him. When he finally learns that he unwittingly fulfilled the very prophecy he spent his life trying to avoid, Oedipus does not submit to the gods or surrender his agency. He does their bidding—he "drive[s] the corruption from the land"—but he takes the situation one step further by deciding to blind himself first. When the Chorus asks what "superhuman power" drove him to commit such a horrible act, Oedipus exclaims, "The hand that struck my eyes was mine, / mine alone—no one else— / I did it all myself!" Oedipus does not seek to escape his punishment, but he does assert his right to exact that punishment as he sees fit. Even as he is brought low, Oedipus refuses to relinquish power over his own life and body.

Oedipus was saddled with a terrible curse through no fault of his own. In this sense, his fate is arbitrary. His actions, however, are not. Oedipus cannot escape the specific points of the prophecy, but that prophecy only determines the limits of his freedom. Within its scope, he is free to act as he chooses. In this sense, Oedipus resembles his daughter Antigone, who must decide whether to exercise her personal choice and bury her brother, Polynices, despite the fact that the law will certainly condemn her to death. Though *Oedipus the King* and *Antigone* were written over two millennia ago, they continue to offer us models of how individuals can and must exercise their freedoms of choice, even in the face of such powerful forces as law, fate, or the gods.

GLOSSARY OF LITERARY TERMS

ANTAGONIST

The entity that acts to frustrate the goals of the *protagonist*. The antagonist is usually another *character* but may also be a non-human force.

ANTIHERO / ANTIHEROINE

A *protagonist* who is not admirable or who challenges notions of what should be considered admirable.

CHARACTER

A person, animal, or any other thing with a personality that appears in a *narrative*.

CLIMAX

The moment of greatest intensity in a text or the major turning point in the *plot*.

CONFLICT

The central struggle that moves the *plot* forward. The conflict can be the *protagonist*'s struggle against fate, nature, society, or another person.

FIRST-PERSON POINT OF VIEW

A literary style in which the *narrator* tells the story from his or her own *point of view* and refers to himself or herself as "I." The narrator may be an active participant in the story or just an observer.

HERO / HEROINE

The principal *character* in a literary work or *narrative*.

IMAGERY

Language that brings to mind sense-impressions, representing things that can be seen, smelled, heard, tasted, or touched.

MOTIF

A recurring idea, structure, contrast, or device that develops or informs the major *themes* of a work of literature.

NARRATIVE

A story.

LITERARY ANALYSIS

NARRATOR
The person (sometimes a *character*) who tells a story; the *voice* assumed by the writer. The narrator and the author of the work of literature are not the same person.

PLOT
The arrangement of the events in a story, including the sequence in which they are told, the relative emphasis they are given, and the causal connections between events.

POINT OF VIEW
The *perspective* that a *narrative* takes toward the events it describes.

PROTAGONIST
The main *character* around whom the story revolves.

SETTING
The location of a *narrative* in time and space. Setting creates mood or atmosphere.

SUBPLOT
A secondary *plot* that is of less importance to the overall story but may serve as a point of contrast or comparison to the main plot.

SYMBOL
An object, *character*, figure, or color that is used to represent an abstract idea or concept. Unlike an *emblem,* a symbol may have different meanings in different contexts.

SYNTAX
The way the words in a piece of writing are put together to form lines, phrases, or clauses; the basic structure of a piece of writing.

THEME
A fundamental and universal idea explored in a literary work.

TONE
The author's attitude toward the subject or *characters* of a story or poem or toward the reader.

VOICE
An author's individual way of using language to reflect his or her own personality and attitudes. An author communicates voice through *tone, diction,* and *syntax.*

A NOTE ON PLAGIARISM

Plagiarism—presenting someone else's work as your own—rears its ugly head in many forms. Many students know that copying text without citing it is unacceptable. But some don't realize that even if you're not quoting directly, but instead are paraphrasing or summarizing, *it is plagiarism* unless you cite the source.

Here are the most common forms of plagiarism:

- Using an author's phrases, sentences, or paragraphs without citing the source
- Paraphrasing an author's ideas without citing the source
- Passing off another student's work as your own

How do you steer clear of plagiarism? You should *always* acknowledge all words and ideas that aren't your own by using quotation marks around verbatim text or citations like footnotes and endnotes to note another writer's ideas. For more information on how to give credit when credit is due, ask your teacher for guidance or visit www.sparknotes.com.

Review & Resources

Quiz

1. Which of the three Theban plays was probably written last?

    A. *Oedipus at Colonus*
    B. No one knows
    C. *Oedipus the King*
    D. *Antigone*

2. How many children does Oedipus have?

    A. 2
    B. 3
    C. 4
    D. None

3. In *Oedipus the King*, whose murder must be avenged to end the plague in Thebes?

    A. Creon's
    B. Polybus's
    C. Laius's
    D. Polynices'

4. Which of Oedipus's children does not appear in *Oedipus at Colonus*?

    A. Antigone
    B. Polynices
    C. Eteocles
    D. Ismene

5. What does the name "Oedipus" mean?

    A. "Incest-monger"
    B. "King of Thebes"
    C. "Swollen foot"
    D. "Blinded by Fate"

6. Which of the three Theban plays was probably written first?

    A. No one knows
    B. *Oedipus the King*
    C. *Oedipus at Colonus*
    D. *Antigone*

7. In what country was Oedipus raised?

    A. Colonus
    B. Thebes
    C. Corinth
    D. Athens

8. In which play does Tiresias not appear?

    A. *Oedipus the King*
    B. *Antigone*
    C. He appears in all three.
    D. *Oedipus at Colonus*

9. What sentence does Creon impose upon Antigone for violating his edict prohibiting Polynices' burial?

    A. She must be hanged.
    B. Her eyes must be stabbed out.
    C. She must be banished.
    D. She must be buried alive.

10. What is Creon's relationship to Jocasta?

    A. Brother
    B. Father
    C. Son
    D. Uncle

11. What does Oedipus use to stab out his own eyes?

    A. Knives
    B. Sticks
    C. The brooches from Jocasta's robe
    D. The horns of a sacrificial bull

12. From whose curse did Oedipus rescue Thebes?

    A.   The Sphinx's

    B.   Laius's

    C.   Apollo's

    D.   Creon's

13. Who speaks last in each of the Theban plays?

    A.   Ismene

    B.   Creon

    C.   A messenger

    D.   The Chorus

14. Whom was Antigone meant to marry?

    A.   Polynices

    B.   Haemon

    C.   Eteocles

    D.   She was not meant to be married.

15. Which god did Athenian theatrical performances celebrate?

    A.   Athena

    B.   Zeus

    C.   Dionysus

    D.   Sophocles

16. Which of the following characters remains alive throughout the three Theban plays?

    A.   Oedipus

    B.   Creon

    C.   Antigone

    D.   Jocasta

17. Where was Laius killed?

    A.   On a one-lane bridge

    B.   Between a rock and a hard place

    C.   In the mountains of Corinth

    D.   At a three-way crossroads

18. In *Oedipus at Colonus*, how does Creon attempt to coerce Oedipus to return to Thebes?

   A.   He kidnaps his daughters.
   B.   He bribes Theseus.
   C.   He threatens war with Polynices.
   D.   He promises Oedipus new eyes.

19. What does Oedipus prophecy about Polynices and Eteocles?

   A.   They will rule Thebes together.
   B.   They will die at each other's hands.
   C.   They will be betrayed by Creon.
   D.   They will sleep with their mother and kill their father.

20. Who is the last remaining survivor of Oedipus's family?

   A.   Ismene
   B.   Antigone
   C.   Oedipus
   D.   Eteocles

21. Which of the following deaths occurs onstage?

   A.   Oedipus's
   B.   Jocasta's
   C.   Antigone's
   D.   None of these deaths occurs onstage.

22. What does Creon do just before he finds Antigone dead?

   A.   Banishes Tiresias
   B.   Argues with his wife, Eurydice
   C.   Gives Polynices a proper burial
   D.   Visits the oracle

23. What is the name of the character who helps Oedipus in *Oedipus at Colonus*?

   A.   Merope
   B.   Polybus
   C.   Theseus
   D.   Cadmus

24. Which of the following characters does not commit suicide?

    A. Antigone
    B. Ismene
    C. Haemon
    D. Eurydice

25. To whom do the woods belong where *Oedipus at Colonus* takes place?

    A. Euripides
    B. The Eumenides
    C. Eteocles
    D. Theseus

SUGGESTIONS FOR FURTHER READING

ADAMS, S. M. *Sophocles the Playwright*. Toronto: University of Toronto Press, 1957.

GELLIE, G. H. *Sophocles: A Reading*. Carlton, Victoria, AUS: Melbourne University Press, 1972.

KITTO, H. D. F. *Greek Tragedy: A Literary Study*. Oxford, UK: Routledge, reprint edition 2002.

KNOX, BERNARD. *Oedipus at Thebes: Sophocles' Tragic Hero and His Time*. New Haven, CT: Yale University Press, 1998.

LATTIMORE, RICHMOND. *The Poetry of Greek Tragedy*. Baltimore: Johns Hopkins University Press, reprint edition 2003.

SEGAL, CHARLES. *Oedipus Tyrannus: Tragic Heroism and the Limits of Knowledge*. New York: Oxford University Press, 2000.

TAPLIN, OLIVER. *Greek Tragedy in Action*. Oxford, UK: Routledge, reprint edition, 2002.

WEBSTER, T. B. L. *An Introduction to Sophocles*. Oxford, UK: Clarendon Press, 1936.

WINNINGTON-INGRAM, R. P. *Sophocles: An Interpretation*. Cambridge, UK: Cambridge University Press, reprint edition 2002.